Ironwork Today 3

Inside and Out

Jeffrey B. Snyder

Dedication

To my family and friends, who keep me centered and make life a joy.

Acknowledgments

I wish to thank all the artists everywhere who submitted work and shared information for this book. Your enthusiasm is inspirational, as is the dedication to your art. The Artist Blacksmith's Association of North America, ABANA, and ABANA's chapters across the United States and Canada have been supportive to this ongoing series.

Other Schiffer Books By The Author:
Art Jewelry Today 2. 9780764330650. $50.00
Art Jewelry Today 3. 9780764338830. $50.00
Ironwork Today 2: Inside and Out. 9780764330643. $50.00

Other Schiffer Books on Related Subjects:
Architectural Ironwork. Dona Z. Meilach. 076431324X. $49.95
Art Jewelry Today. Dona Z. Meilach. 0764317660. $50.00
Decorative & Sculptural Ironwork: Tools, Techniques & Inspiration. Dona Z. Meilach. 9780764307904. $34.99
Decorative Architectural Ironwork. Diana Stuart. 0764321927. $39.95
Ironwork Today: Inside & Out. Dona Z. Meilach. 0764323903. $49.95

Library of Congress Control Number: 2011934788

Book and cover designed by: Bruce Waters
Type set in Arrus BT/Zurich BT

ISBN: 978-0-7643-3876-2
Printed in Hong Kong

Schiffer Books are available at special discounts for bulk purchases for sales promotions or premiums. Special editions, including personalized covers, corporate imprints, and excerpts can be created in large quantities for special needs. For more information contact the publisher:

Published by Schiffer Publishing Ltd.
4880 Lower Valley Road
Atglen, PA 19310
Phone: (610) 593-1777; Fax: (610) 593-2002
E-mail: Info@schifferbooks.com

For the largest selection of fine reference books on this and related subjects, please visit our website at **www.schifferbooks.com**
We are always looking for people to write books on new and related subjects. If you have an idea for a book, please contact us at proposals@schifferbooks.com

This book may be purchased from the publisher.
Include $5.00 for shipping.
Please try your bookstore first.
You may write for a free catalog.

In Europe, Schiffer books are distributed by
Bushwood Books
6 Marksbury Ave.
Kew Gardens
Surrey TW9 4JF England
Phone: 44 (0) 20 8392 8585; Fax: 44 (0) 20 8392 9876
E-mail: info@bushwoodbooks.co.uk
Website: www.bushwoodbooks.co.uk

Contents

Introduction

This volume presents a sampling from the impressive range of artwork created almost entirely during the latter half of the first decade of the twenty-first century. The artists are presented alphabetically, allowing readers to review the range of each artist's work together. The artists speak for themselves about their artwork, their sources of inspiration, and their approaches to their work.

Jeff Fetty. *Photo: Gefeti*

Shawn Lovell

The artist blacksmiths presented here work alone or in collaboration with others. They create original works of art, which are sold to clients directly or through galleries. Some of their artwork ends up in museums, either on display in exhibits or as part of the museum's structure itself. Their enduring works are created in a range of metals. They use a wide variety of equipment ranging from anvils and hammers to hydraulic presses and laser cutters. These artist blacksmiths create everything from fire tools and furniture to intricate railings and monumental sculptures. Their work will surprise you, especially if this is your first introduction to this world. The range of their innovative creations will challenge your preconceived notions of the blacksmith's art.

John Boyd Smith. Chandelier, Pool Table Lighting, and Balcony.

John T.G. Aakesson

Springfield, Virginia

Artist's Statement

My work stems from two different sources of inspiration. The first source comes from incorporating the human figure into my work. The study of the body's natural movement has allowed for the abstractions that appear in my work. The second source is found in using shapes and forms found in nature to focus my idea of modern design. As humans commune with nature, the shapes around us naturally affect us on a subconscious level. I believe that all designs will be able to fit into any living space and not break the harmony that previously existed there.

Individual Artwork

John T.G. Aakesson. Bent figure side table. Forged, bent, and welded steel, leather, and glass. 37″ h x 60″ w x 18″ d.

John T.G. Aakesson. Broken circle table. Bent steel, lacquered, and glass. 29.5″ h x 36″ w x 21″ d.

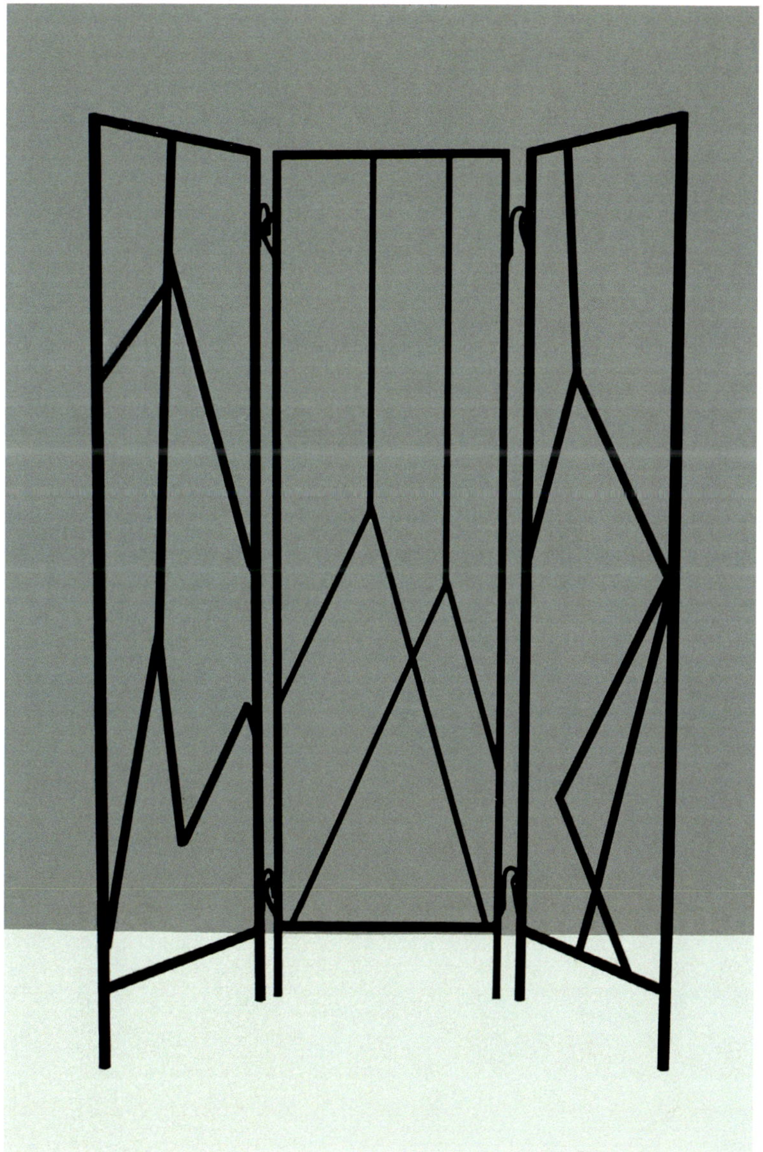

John T.G. Aakesson. Figured Screen. Welded steel, lacquered, and glass. 72″ h x 66″ w x 1.25″ d.

John T.G. Aakesson. Square spiral coffee table. Welded steel, lacquered, and glass. 16" h x 42" w x 72" d.

John T.G. Aakesson

John T.G. Aakesson. Zig zag chair. Cut welded steel, cherry wood lacquered. 40" h x 21.5" w x 19" d.

John T.G. Aakesson. Stair chair. Cut welded steel, cherry wood, and French polish. 40" h x 21.5" w x 19" d.

John T.G. Aakesson

Sean Ahern

Charleston, South Carolina, sean@ahernsanvil.com

Artist's Statement

Growing up in Charleston, South Carolina, I have been surrounded my entire life by Lowcountry landscapes like marsh grass, Spanish moss, and architecture steeped in hundreds of years of history. Ironwork is an integral element in many of the historical homes here, and I've always admired our celebrated blacksmiths like Philip Simmons for carrying on the design traditions of this beautiful city. I definitely draw inspiration for my designs from my surroundings, and enjoy working with clients who have a connection to the natural elements of the Lowcountry, like cattails, grasses, and palm fronds, and want these things worked into their designs.

I derive so much of my creative energy from organic landscapes of all kinds, not just in the Lowcountry. I get ideas and inspiration by considering the texture, growth, and movement of all life forms and nature, like how the wind moves through the grass, the ebb and flow of the ocean, and the balance of rolling hills.

Individual Artwork

Bar Lamps

Lighting designed for the Hilton Resort on Hilton Head Island, South Carolina. The lights have an acrylic defuser.

Sean Ahern. Bar Lamps. Forged and fabricated. Steel and wire mesh.

Table Base

I designed and built this table base as a donation to Habitat for Humanity, for an art show titled "Bird House." This base was all forged steel, with the bird forged out of an old hammer I had in the shop.

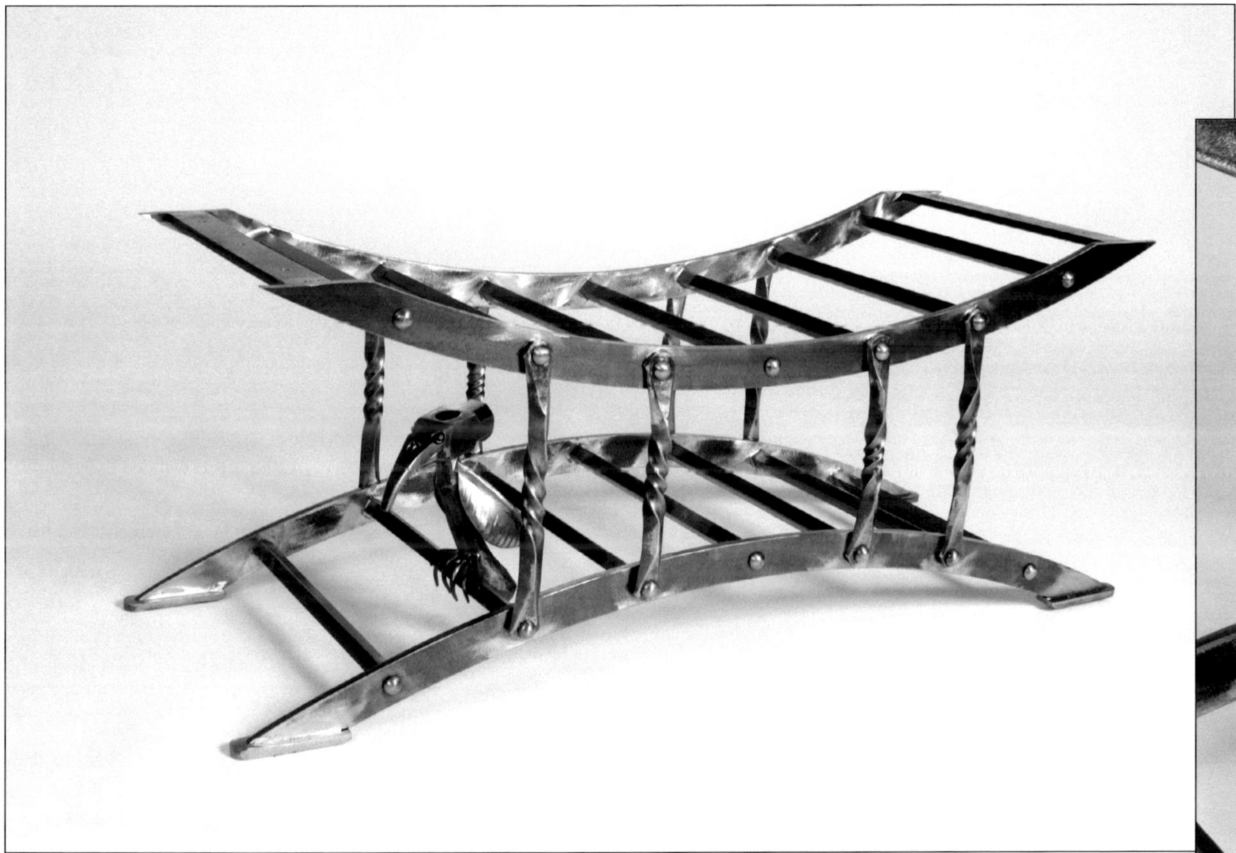

Sean Ahern. Table Base. 2006. Forged. Steel.

Bronze Fountain

Sean Ahern. Bronze Fountain. 2006. Forged, formed, and fabricated. Trellis: solid silicon bronze; bowl/base: bronze sheet.

Sculpture

I was asked to come up with something that the people of the Lowcountry of South Carolina could relate to. I was born here in Charleston. I grew up seeing old women weaving sweetgrass baskets on the side of the road and in the streets. When they start a basket, it starts off as a fan of grass. This sculpture presents an abstract depiction of the beginning of a sweetgrass basket. Unfortunately, the project had been put off at the time of this writing. I forged this piece on a much smaller scale at the end of 2009.

Sean Ahern. Sculpture. 2009. Forged. Steel. Outdoors sculpture for a large public space in Charleston, South Carolina.

Fire Basket

The client was looking for something elegant for their fireplace. They wanted andirons. They also wanted to keep the fireplace looking clean.

Sean Ahern. Fire Basket. 2009. Forged. Steel.

Fire Screen

This was designed for a client whose home is among the South Carolina marshlands.

Sean Ahern. Fire Screen. 2010. Forged. Steel.

Joseph Anderson

Walnut Cove, North Carolina, ironjpa@triad.rr.com

Artist's Statement

The series I have been working on for the last four years is based on abstracted human figures, most often done as singles or pairs. Motion, emotion, interaction, and dance are the concepts that are most often manifested within this body of work. I find form and volume by applying calligraphic elements in different sizes and configurations to each individual piece.

Individual Artwork

Joseph Anderson. *Dancing Under The Stars*. 2007. Forged steel, paint. 19″ x 7″ x 7″.

Joseph Anderson. *Watching Over.* 2007. Forged steel, paint. 23″ x 7″ x 9″.

Joseph Anderson. *Finish Line.* 2009. Forged steel, paint. 22″ x 12″ x 9″.

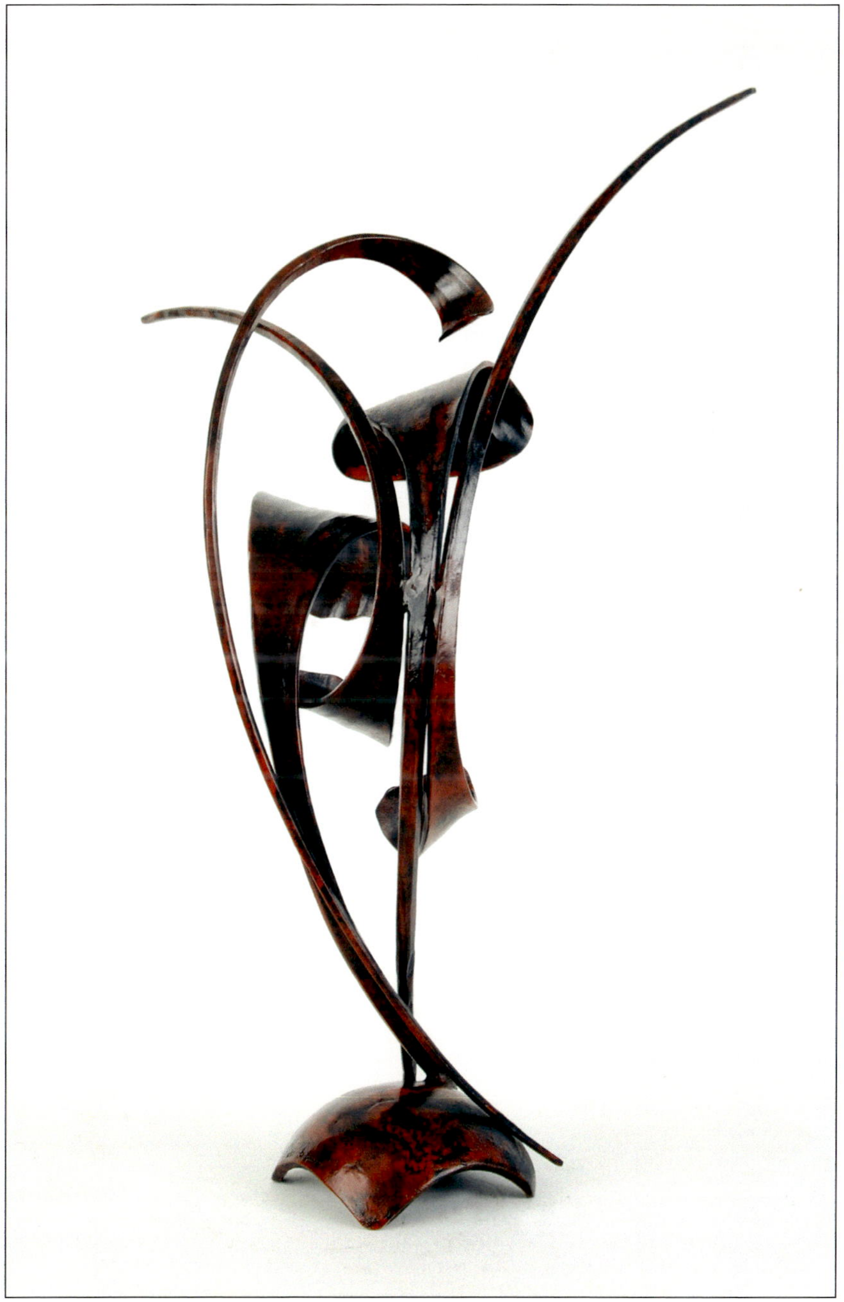

Joseph Anderson. *Rock.* 2009. Forged steel, paint. 22″ x 14″ x 11″.

Frank Annighofer

Roscoe, Montana, frank@woodandironworks.com

Artist's Statement

I consider myself a minimalist, trying to achieve as much as possible with as little as possible. Forging iron the classic way does not take much more than iron, fire, and inspiration. If tools are necessary, they can be made utilizing the same iron, fire, and inspiration. For my designs, I try to focus on the overall theme and aesthetics. This leaves some room for the observer to do his or her own interpretation.

Individual Artwork

Wild and Free

The task was to create a life-sized, rearing Indian horse sculpture. It was supposed to be light, yet strong. Local artist Glenn L. Smith made the first sketch. Initial trials building a solid structure with "steel skin" did not give the dynamic that one would associate with a wild horse. In time, I came up with a more abstract frame structure. After playing with a wire bend 6 inch high model, the final sculpture was forged and fabricated out of 1 1/4 and 1 inch round steel and copper flat bar. The result is a sculpture light enough to wave in the wind, yet strong enough to withstand severe winter Chinook winds. It is a symbol of wildness and freedom. Copper rivets attaching the mane remind viewers of braiding. Twists make that mane glitter in the sun.

Frank Annighofer. *Wild and Free.* Horse sculpture. 2007. Forged and fabricated. Iron and copper. 12 x 7 x 3 feet. Private residence, Roscoe, Montana. (right and opposite page)

Stair Railing

This rail combines log posts with hand forged mild steel panels. Wood is the strong component in this design; iron is the weak and playful element. This creates a dynamic and also blends well with a log rail continuation around the deck. Posts are 8-inch fire killed lodgepole pine. Rails are made from 1 inch and 5/8 inch round steel. Seven rail segments add up to 50 total feet. The design idea came from an old 1900s window grille in Hamburg, Germany. It was completely hand forged, employing no electric welding. And so is the new rail. Half penny scrolls are hand hammered from round stock and assembled with collars. Tenons are forged to the picket ends, riveted through punched holes in the top and bottom rails. Rails are polished and clear coated with an acrylic lacquer. Annette Lavalette, Frank's wife, forged all of this project's small scrolls.

Frank Annighofer. Stair Railing, for a log home. 2008. Hand forged with traditional joinery. Mild steel. Private residence, Roscoe, Montana.

Pool Area Banister

This rail was supposed to have its own appeal, without distracting from the magnificent landscape around it. The design was to be straight and functional, reflecting organic vines and leaves. The client also loved the color of copper. The result was a combination of scrolls with curly leaf ends and arrowhead pickets. The leaves were forge copper plated. Repeating the copper theme with rivets attaching the picket helps bridge the style gap from curly to straight. Frames are forged from 1 inch square and 1 x 1 1/2 inch flat bar for strengths. The fill is 3/4, 5/8, and 1/2 inch stock to provide as much view through the banister as possible. All joinery is traditional, using tenons, rivets, and split end collars. The project consists of 6 banisters of about 35 feet total.

Frank Annighofer. Pool Area Banisters. 2009. Hand forged with all traditional joinery. Mild steel with copper accents. Private residence, Red Lodge, Montana.

Austin Metal Authority

Austin, Texas, metalmantis@gmail.com

Artist's Statement

In the first decade of the twenty-first century, civilization is being forced to come to terms with the exploitive path it has been on since the onset of the Industrial Revolution. Humanity at-large, as well as governments and politicians, seems more and more at the mercy of Big Business, which owns—and controls—an ever-shrinking pool of resources. Hydra City, based on the Lernaean Hydra of Greek mythology, is a symbol of this struggle.

The myth of the Hydra, a seven-headed beast that guarded the entrance to the Underworld, is told as one of Heracles'—adopted in Roman mythology as Hercules—Twelve Labors. His struggle to slay the beast, who re-grew two heads for each one Heracles removed, was ultimately managed when his nephew, Iolaus, discovered using a firebrand to cauterize the necks would prevent new heads from forming, thereby allowing Heracles to bring about its demise.

Hydra City, seven forged hydra heads dominating over a burning, modern-day cityscape, represents the sense of hopelessness aroused when combating a force that seems insurmountable. It also suggests that by working together—just as Heracles and Iolaus, and the sculpture's seven artists did—humanity can overcome the forces-that-be and create an alternate path for our collective future.

Individual Artwork

Austin Metal Authority Artists: Robert Abdallah, Colby Brinkman, Troy Defrates, Brady Foster, Rebekah Frank, Colin McIntyre, and Haley Woodward. *Hydra City.* Sculpture. 2010. Forged and fabricated mild steel. Reclaimed mild steel. 36" l x 36" w x 60" h. *Photos: Patrick Bertolino*

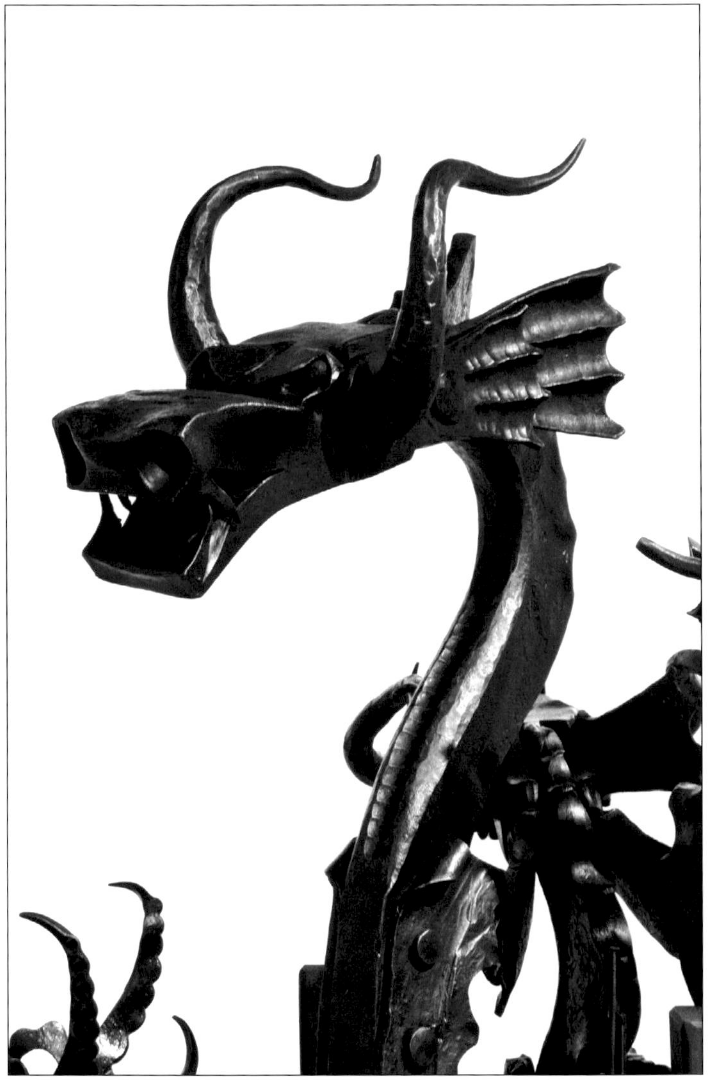

Lee W. Badger

Hedgesville, West Virginia, lee@heybadger.com

Artist's Statement

Many artist-blacksmiths think of furniture making in terms of scrolls and ornaments, forgings and "wrought iron." However, I focus on furniture design and the steel material itself instead of craft traditions. I also feel free to use any advanced technology or ancient technique that can take me toward my creative goals.

The traditional and functional forms of furniture have familiar and satisfying sculptural qualities, and I like to work within that realm. I'm not drawn to making sculpture with a furniture purpose or furniture with a fundamentally sculptural role. I think a piece of furniture only becomes a work of art when the design and the craftsmanship inspire each other and meld into a single accomplishment.

Individual Artwork

Tubendstil Tables

For *Tubendstil Tables,* I plasma cut, hot form, and MIG-weld them from sections of 6" x 6" steel tube and 1/4" plate. Then they are filed, joined, and finished, each one crafted individually or in matching sets.

Although this design requires contemporary tools and techniques for execution, it reflects the *Jugendstil* style developed by German and Austrian Art Nouveau craftsmen more than 100 years ago. *Tubendstil Tables* slightly resemble an oak tray table made by Herman Obrist in 1898, now in the Bavarian National Museum.

In developing this design, I found the opportunity for a modern twist. The *Tubendstil Table* is reversible. It can be inverted and both ways are right side up – the design carries through in either orientation. Each position demonstrates appealing shape, line, and proportion equally well.

Lee W. Badger. *Tubendstil Table.* 2006. Hot worked 6 x 6 structural steel square tube with black oxide finish and ceramic tile top. 26" h x 14" w x 14" d.

Stone Top Tables

The *Stone Top Table* design floats a stone top on a steel framework, expressing strength without heaviness. Steel has its origins in stone, and both are durable, strong, and heavy. Stock steel is consistent and remarkable in its structural strength and workability, but stone has variable characteristics and each piece can be individually unique. This design concept emphasizes the contrast between these two generally similar materials by combining singular stone tabletops with a strong and light steel support.

Stone Top Tables strike a balance between heavy and light. The table legs are cut and crafted from structural steel stock commonly known as "angle iron," and 1/2" rod forms the frame and stone supports. Carefully shaped and finished welds join the exposed corners of the frame and seamless hidden interior welds join the legs to the frame. This creates a strong supporting base with a light and uplifted appearance.

Lee W. Badger. *Stone Top Table*. 2008. Welded, cut, and filed steel angle and rod with black oxide patina and Pennsylvania flagstone top. 18" h x 24" w x 18" d.

Knotted Tables

The Knotted Table design came out of a traditional skill building exercise first given to me as an apprentice artist-blacksmith. It requires expert hot working control to intertwine four steel rods into a tight, symmetrical "knot." When I became interested in furniture design, I modified and adapted this knot bending exercise to form the corners of table frames to hold inset glass tops.

The design has several secrets. To make a symmetrical table, the corner knots must be left and right handed. I make each corner separately and join the sidebars with perfectly finished and hidden MIG welds. Also, I use a gas torch to bend and square the table's knots.

Lee W. Badger. *Knotted Coffee Table.* 2008. Hot worked 1/2" steel rod with brass brushed and enamel rubbed finish, inset 1/2" plate glass top. 18" h x 50" w x 25" d.

Lee W. Badger. *Knotted Table.* 2009. Hot worked 1/2" steel rod with blasted and wire brushed finish, inset 1/2" plate glass top. 18" h x 25 1/2" w x 21" d.

Quadrat-Motif Tables

Many European and American Arts & Crafts designers used the *Quadrat-Motif* – repetitive patterns of squares – to provide a decorative element without creating an excessively ornamental effect. Josef Hoffman and Frank Lloyd Wright frequently used repetitive squares as a design element. Karl Kipp and Dard Hunter often employed the decorative square motif in designs for the Tookay and Roycroft shops. Today, historic *Quadrat-Motif* designs can be seen as contributing precursors to twentieth century Modernism and the International Style.

The Quadrat-Motif Tables are a modern interpretation of these Arts & Crafts influences. The tables are individually crafted from laser cut and hand forged steel.

The finish is a brown oxide patina created directly from the steel surface and fixed with Boston Polish amber paste wax. The tops are 1/2″ bronze plate glass with beveled edges. The inset top design allows alternate tops of wood, stone or composite solid-surface materials.

Lee W. Badger. *Quadrat-Motif Cocktail Table.* 2009. Laser-cut, forged and welded steel with 1/2″ beveled plate glass top. 21″ h x 15″ d.

Lee W. Badger. *Quadrat-Motif Side Tables*. 2009. Laser-cut, forged and welded steel with 1/2″ beveled plate glass top. 26″ h x 25″ w x 25″ d.

William J. Bastas

Del Valle, Texas, wbastas@austincc.edu

Artist's Statement

The art of blacksmithing will live on as long as we continue to teach the tradition while explaining its relevance to those who aspire to learn it. It must be taught thoroughly and painstakingly. However, we also have to allow for interpretation through a contemporary perspective if the art is to thrive beyond historical re-enactments. Although six millennia old, our craft of blacksmithing can be the most novel, expeditious, and fresh resolution to contemporary design and fabrication problems.

Individual Artwork

Screensaver

This hand forged floral composition is a tongue in cheek reference to a computer monitor screen saver. I created this piece to explore forge welding and a stylized approach to traditional forms.

William J. Bastas. *Screensaver*. 2004. Hand forged, forge welded. Forged steel. 24″ h x 30″ w.

Plastic Bag in the Sea

I wanted to utilize the scroll form interpreted in sheet metal to provide a cover for the lights and mica. My design sense is steam punk with a nod toward Arts and Crafts. Technically, the most challenging part is forming sheet metal into flowing compound curves.

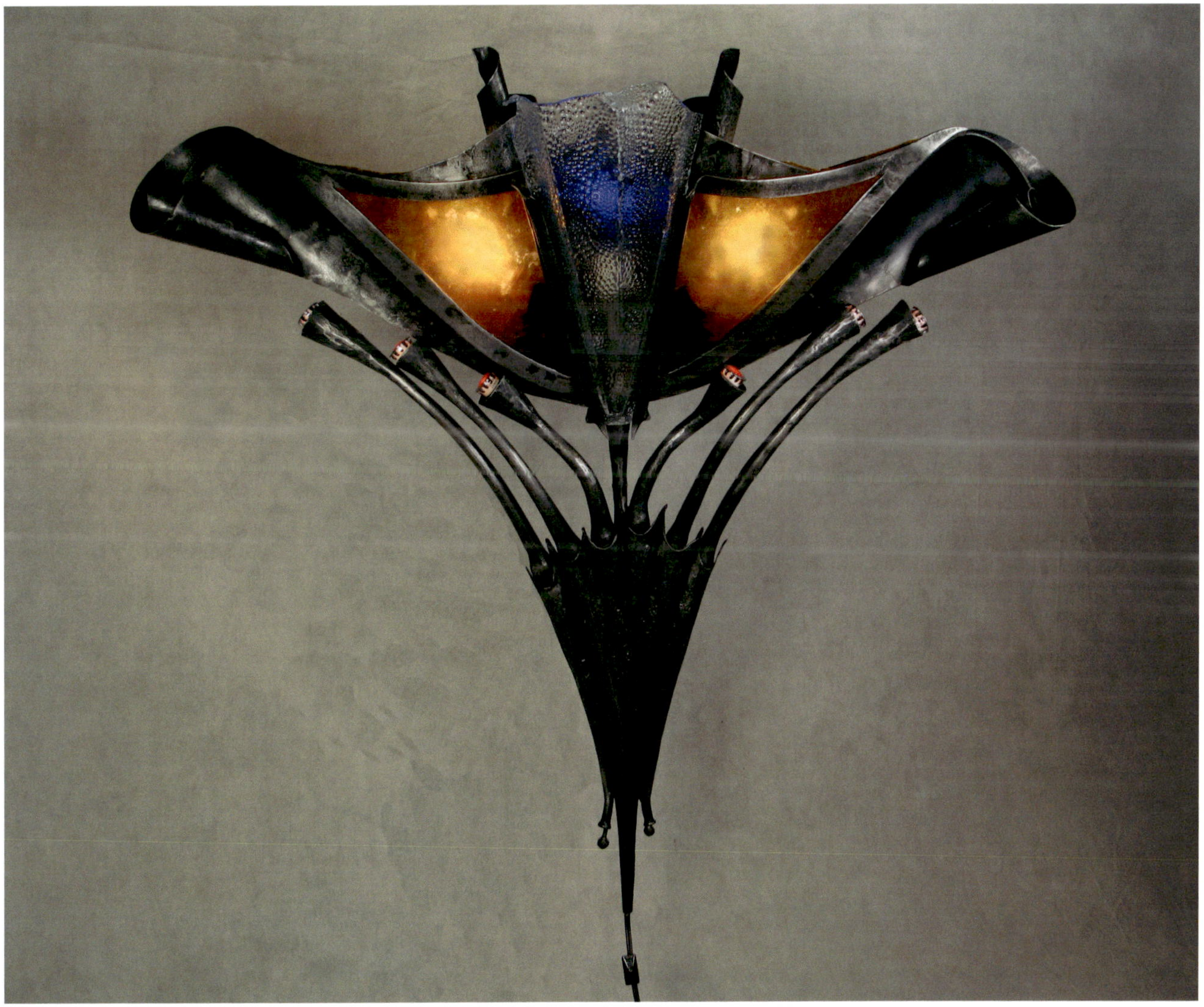

William J. Bastas. *Plastic Bag in the Sea.* Accent Light. Forged and fabricated. Flat bar, sheet metal, slumped glass, and amber mica. 48″ h x 40″ w.

Chicken of the Sea

This Van Erp inspired electrolier is designed to capture the hybrid grace of a starfish/octopus. My intention was to create a feature light that casts warm light below using thin amber mica, and white uplight to bounce off the ceiling. As well, I wanted to have the option of a black light novelty. The marbles inset in the arms are Vaseline glass, harmonizing with the center glass cone's green color.

William J. Bastas. *Chicken of the Sea*. Electrolier. 2006. Forged steel, slumped glass, amber mica, and Vaseline marbles.

Mailbox Post

I designed this composition as a power hammer project for my students to learn drawing, tapering, punching, slitting, upsetting, spreading, veining, and bending. It is all traditionally joined, and meets height—but not breakaway—post office requirements.

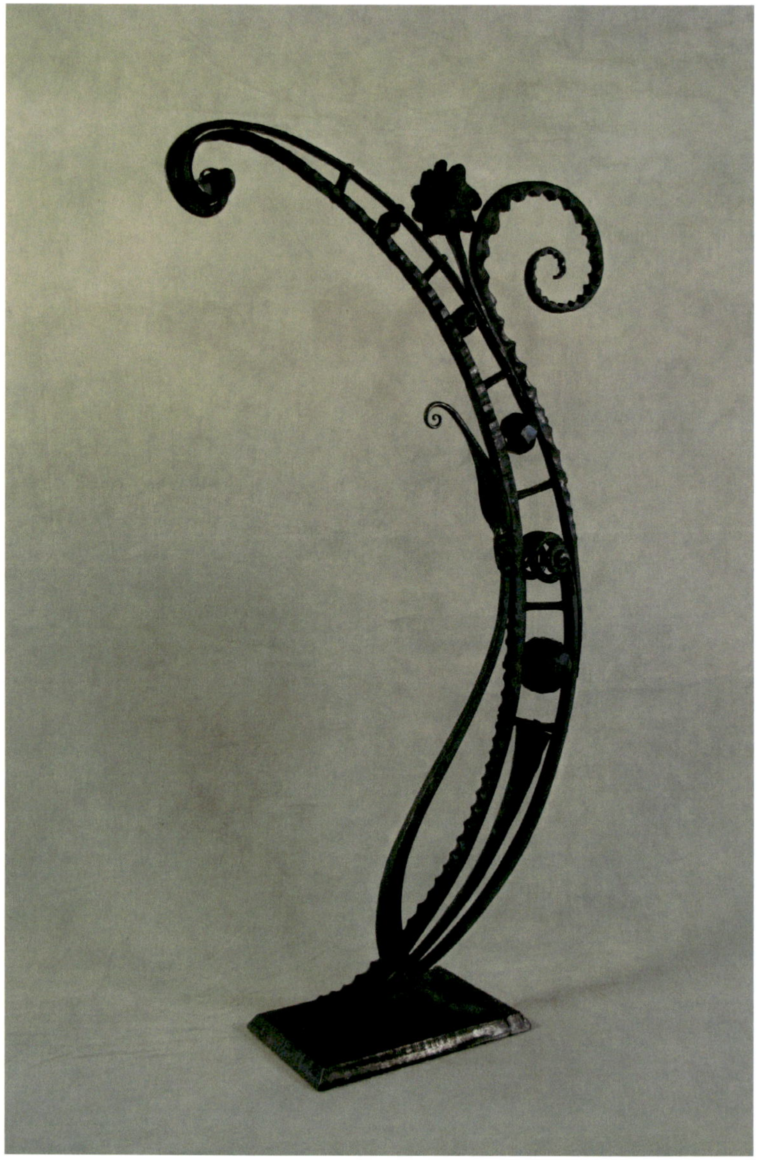

William J. Bastas. Mailbox Post. 2007. Forged steel, traditional joinery. 42″ h x 12″ w.

Shingle Bracket

I designed this bracket to teach my beginning blacksmithing students the skills expected of a journeyman smith, as outlined by Bob Bergman and stated in the ABANA journeyman requirements. The students had the opportunity to see the development of the idea from sketches to finished project. When they were finished with their shingle, the piece symbolically represented the hanging of the shingle, or public statement of intention to open your own business. It is designed utilizing traditional forms of scrolls and joinery, not coincidentally utilizing the proportion system of the golden rectangle.

William J. Bastas. Shingle Bracket. 2007. Forged steel. 27″ h x 18″ w.

Dead Zone

Another assigned project to teach beginning blacksmithing students the skills expected of a journeyman smith, this design utilized the golden proportion, rhythm of threes, and directionality. It was an opportunity also to abstract traditional scroll forms for texture and negative space.

William J. Bastas. Dead Zone. 2009. Forged steel. 36″ h x 24″ w.

Erik Bogner

Tempe, Arizona

Artist's Statement

These pieces explore edged weaponry. Each culture created its own myths, legends, and art around its weaponry. My artwork pays tribute to the historical craft of these cultures and the lore surrounding the weaponry, while forging something that is both timeless and new.

Individual Artwork

Straight Razor

This piece is made from the very first billet of Damascus (pattern welded) steel I ever made and has 384 layers. The goal of this piece was to make a razor that would last so I would not have to buy disposable razors ever again.

Erik Bogner. *Straight Razor*. 2009. Pattern welded steel. Damascus steel, cocobolo wood. 6″ x 1″ x 1″ (closed); 10″ x 1″ x 1″ (fully opened).

Table Setting

The Damascus steel for the fork and spoon is 45 layers. The layers in the knife are unknown because it was salvaged from the same billet as *Failures' Options*.

Erik Bogner. *Table Setting*. Knife, fork, and spoon. 2010. Pattern welded steel. Damascus steel, wood. 6" x 1" (fork and spoon), 8" x 1" (knife).

Failures' Options

This piece is a collection of failed projects and a few rejected items. The original Damascus billet delaminated while I was putting a twist into it so that the blade of this knife is made from what I could salvage from that failed billet. The handle is what remained from a turned bowl that exploded while it was on the lathe. As for the bolster, it is comprised of recycled silver scraps accented with miscut sapphires.

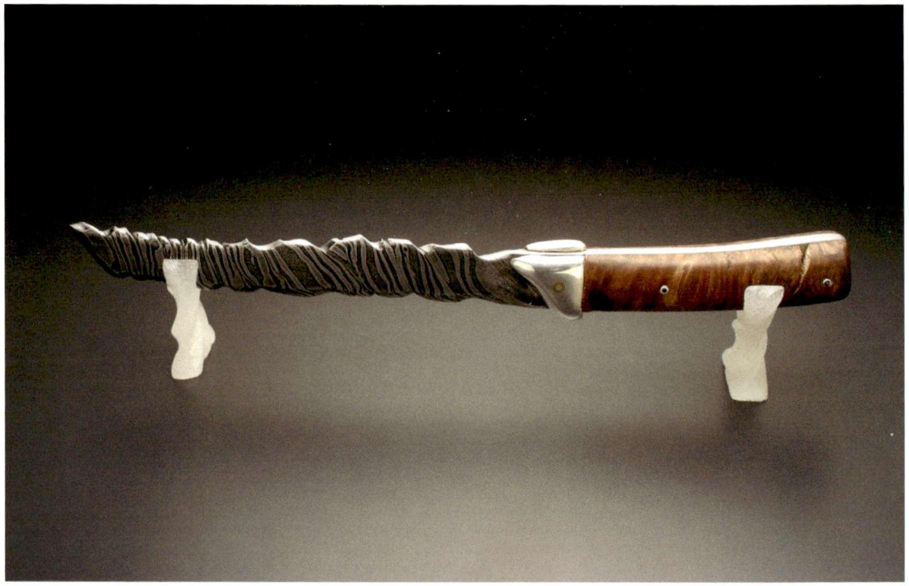

Erik Bogner. *Failures' Options*. Knife. 2010. Pattern welded steel. Damascus steel, silver, wood burl, sapphires. 12" x 1" x 1".

Knife

A study in making a traditional, shaped blade, the blade has just a bit of Damascus forge welded onto it while the rest of the blade and full tang are a high carbon steel. Once satisfied that I could produce a traditional blade style, I embellished the scales with circuit boards salvaged from an old laptop.

Duende Asada Cleaver

The hatchet's handle is 50 layers of Damascus steel while the head is 150 layers. A few friends mentioned that this piece makes an excellent carne asada cleaver. As my current focus is on historical and fantasy edged weaponry, I decided to title the work *Duende Asada Cleaver*, or "roast elf meat clever."

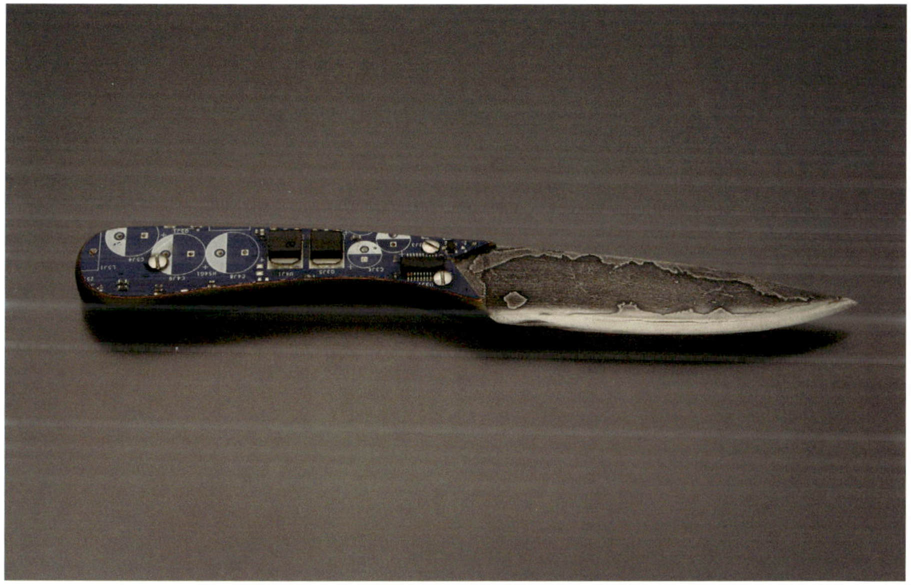

Erik Bogner. *Knife.* 2010. Pattern welded steel. Damascus steel, circuit board. 6" x 1" x 1/2".

Erik Bogner. *Duende Asada Cleaver*. 2010. Pattern welded steel. Damascus steel, leather. 12" x 2 3/4" x 1/4".

Michael Bondi

Richmond, California, michael@michaelbondi.com

Artist's Statement

I have been involved in a dialogue between art, craft, architecture, and function for thirty-three years. My work is focused on wrought metals (blacksmithing) as an artistic expression for ornamentation in architecture, with the challenge of combining artistic creativity with architecture, form, and function. At this time, I am a participant in the revival of the blacksmithing craft. A great deal of study and research in the historical background of the craft has been required, study that has given me a strong foundation for the construction of functional artistic ornamentation for architecture. As many of the projects I've been involved with focused on historical or reproduction architectural metal work, it is the understanding of these forms that has allowed me to introduce more creative and contemporary ideas while still respecting the architecture of the building. I feel this is my responsibility as an artist, respecting the architecture of the past while introducing new ideas, designs, and materials.

My work for the last twenty years has involved the use of mixed metals, bronze, steel, copper, and nickel alloys. This work has allowed me to introduced colors and textures not often seen in contemporary forged ironwork. I have tried to combine these forged and textured materials to create a contrast between smooth and machined surfaces. In conjunction with the three-dimensional forms created by forged metal work one can put more animation and life into the work.

Individual Artwork

Michael Bondi. Bronze Elliptical Stair. Forged bronze. 2 1/4″ oval cap rail with forged and formed 5/8″ square bronze pickets. Bronze stair stringer formed from 1″ x 10″ bronze plate. Patina finish. The stair is three stories, approximately 11′ x 9′ 7″ major and minor radius. (above and opposite page)

Michael Bondi. Entry Door and Grills. Entry door made with forged and riveted bronze, copper, stainless steel, and cast glass. Upper window grills are forged, formed, and riveted bronze. Entry measures 12′ x 8 1/2′; the door measures 3 1/2′ x 8 1/2′.

Michael Bondi. Fireplace Screen. Forged steel fire screen with two doors. 48″ x 34″.

Michael Bondi. Bronze stair railing. Forged, slit drifted, and tenon post. Formed woven panel and textured surface. Forged bronze with custom forged 2 1/4″ custom forged cap rail. All of the grillwork is forged and formed from bronze. Patina finish.

Phillip Bowling

North Hollywood, California, info@nobleforge.com

Individual Artwork

Phillip Bowling. "L" Shaped Fireplace Ensemble. Hand forged. Iron and copper.

Phillip Bowling. Single Panel Fireplace Screen. Hand forged. Steel and copper.

Phillip Bowling. *FIREDOGS!* Grate and andirons. Forged steel.

Phillip Bowling. Leaves, flower, and finishes.

Phillip Bowling. Dining Room Chandelier. Forged steel and pipe, coupled in the middle by two threaded rosettes to conceal the wiring. Hand-rubbed oil finish.

Phillip Bowling. Garden Trellis. Forged steel and copper.

Josh Bowman

Formation Metal Arts, Vista, California, joshbowmanmetalworks@cox.net

Individual Artwork

Arched Entry Door

The internal decorative elements are forged and banded 5/8″ square steel. The glass was hinged with its own weather stripping system and the iron was fixed. A floor installed hydraulic closure controls the door's movement. Since this was for a beach house, the door was hot dipped galvanized with a two-part epoxy base coat and a two-part polyurethane topcoat. This glazed entry door is 4′ wide by 8′ tall. Private Residence in Del Mar, California.

Josh Bowman. Arched Entry Door. *Photos: Maria Bowman*

Wine Cellar Doors

Grillwork is forged 1/2″ x 1″ solid steel with bands and is hinged to allow glass cleaning. The door has a hydraulic closure. All surfaces have heavy forged texture with a patina finish that is sealed and waxed. Private Residence in Rancho Santa Fe, California.

Josh Bowman. Wine Cellar Doors. *Photos: Maria Bowman*

Christina Boy

Orange, Virginia, setaina@gmail.com

Artist's Statement

As children our parents and teachers constantly chastised us for rocking on chair legs and squirming in our seats. I believe the human body was not meant to stand or sit still all the time. I believe that the body is meant to move, act, and interact. By setting furniture on rockers, the body is subconsciously starting to interact with it—moving, swaying, and rocking with it.

Furthermore, the rocking motion has numerous connotations. We were rocked to sleep, nursed in a rocking chair, played on rocking playground equipment—from rocking horses and see-saws to swings and those fun seats on springs. Now, as adults, we have office chairs that tilt and rock, we rock the boats we sit in, we rock out to music, and our confidence can be severely rocked by shocking news and events.

All in all I believe that there are not enough rocking things in this often too serious and static world. I want to see more of them exist.

Individual Artwork

Mezza Luna

I learned TIG-welding on this piece, as well as working in sheet metal. It is a rocking bench that can either be used by 3 people side by side, or people seated like on a see-saw, bringing out the child in you. Or you can just having a pleasant conversation with someone special across from you.

Christina Boy. *Mezza Luna*. Rocking Bench. 2009. Hollow form, TIG-welded, patina: ferric nitrate. Sheet metal. 72″ w x 22″ d x 21″ h. *Photos: Tim Barnwell*

Limette

A single little stool to rock out on and enjoy life, or sit and quietly contemplate issues at hand as you sway back and forth, side to side.

Christina Boy. *Limette*. Stool. 2009. Angle iron and sheet metal formed on a hydraulic press, TIG-welded, finish: outside gun-blue patina, inside automotive paint. 24" w x 23" d x 21" h. *Photo: Tim Barnwell*

Wandlung

This mixed media sculptural rocking stool captures some transitional and transformational experiences I have been coming across in my work and life over the past year. Two different entities become one; two materials come together, forming one. In *Wandlung*, the idea was "transition," moving inherent qualities from one material and applying them to another, uniting dark and light, ridged and soft, steel and wood. Many experiences take us back and forth in life; these experiences have happened more lately, shaking up my life as I have been discovering steel and how I can combine it with wood.

Christina Boy. *Wandlung.* Rocking Stool. 2009. Formed by hand and hydraulic press, ferric chloride patina; Arkansas pine: bent lamination, curf cut and bent again; seat: upholstered. Angle iron and sheet metal. 36" w x 19" d x 22" h. *Photo: Jocelyn Howard*

Scott Cawood

Sharpsburg, Maryland, cawood@cawoodart.com

Artist's Statement

My work is a reflection of how the world works, looks, and feels to me, of the everyday discourse I see as visual celebrations and contradictions. This leads to steel portraits of long past Bluesmen wrought from discarded heating oil tanks, the pitted flesh hammered deep with the emotions they evoke. Elegant and alive organic forms are born from pieces of hard-edged industrial detritus.

I use steel, especially scrap steel, as my medium because I feel steel's quailities and limitations best reflect outwardly what defines me inwardly. Scrap steel has no equal in expressing my obsession with the idea of transformation. I started using scrap steel because it was cheap and everywhere. I understood that just under that thin layer of rust lay steel longing to be rediscovered.

Individual Artwork

Bukka and *Furry*

Bukka and *Furry* are the first two sculptures in my series celebrating the Mississippi Delta Bluesmen. I was recently inspired to bring a strong emotional element to my work and realized the human face was the most effective way to accomplish that. It took two years of studying anatomy and developing my process to achieve the desired results.

I chose Blues musicians because I believe their music is art as practiced in its purest form. It is an undiluted reflection of their unique cultural experience, which is loved and understood universally. These artists lived very difficult lives, fighting poverty and prejudice. Despite that, or because of it, they managed to create and expand an original art form. I see them as unsung heroes.

I first sketch my subject to break down the inherant shapes of the face. I then create a substructure out of 1/4" steel rod based on my sketch to lay out those requirements and cut patterns taken from that substructure out of sections of derelict oil tanks, used for their context, availability, thickness, and texture. Raising and shaping each section with a hammer and anvil, I then weld them together onto the substructure. The finish is burnt used motor oil and sealed with polyurethane.

Scott Cawood. *Bukka.* Sculpture. 2009. Forged & welded; burnt oil finish; sealed with polyurethane. Derelict steel heating oil tank, 1/4" steel rod. 16" h x 14" w x 15" d. *Photos: Michael Davis (above and opposite)*

Scott Cawood. *Furry.* Sculpture. 2010. Forged & welded; burnt oil finish, sealed with polyurethane. Derelict steel heating oil tank, 1/4″ steel rod. 18″ h x 15″ w x 16″ d. *Photos: Michael Davis*

Michael Leo Chmielewski

Murphysboro, Illinois, powerhammer6@gmail.com

Artist's Statement

Machines are brought to life by human interaction, whether it is interfacing with the machine or creating it. In this body of work, fluid juxtapositions of extremely different materials and techniques is one of the focuses. Utilizing contemporary materials and forged steel together, the results are playful and intimidating objects that address the potential absurdities between the two elements physically, historically, and technically. This work is also addressing the object and the space, but zeroing in on the theatrical nature of human interaction with art in a very direct manner.

Individual Artwork

Michael Leo Chmielewski. *Confidential #1.* Forged and fabricated. Mild steel, coil spring, brass, copper. 24″ x 8″ x 18″.

Michael Leo Chmielewski. *Confidential #2.* Forged, machined, and fabricated. Mild steel and brass. 8″ x 8″ x 8″.

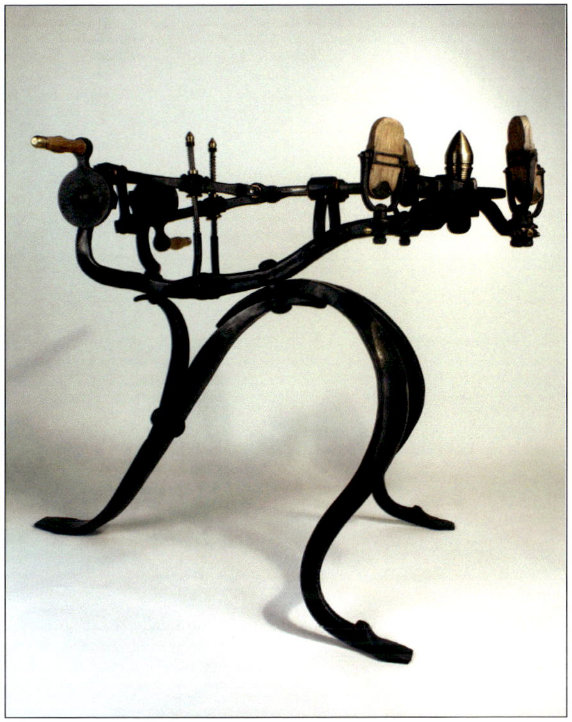

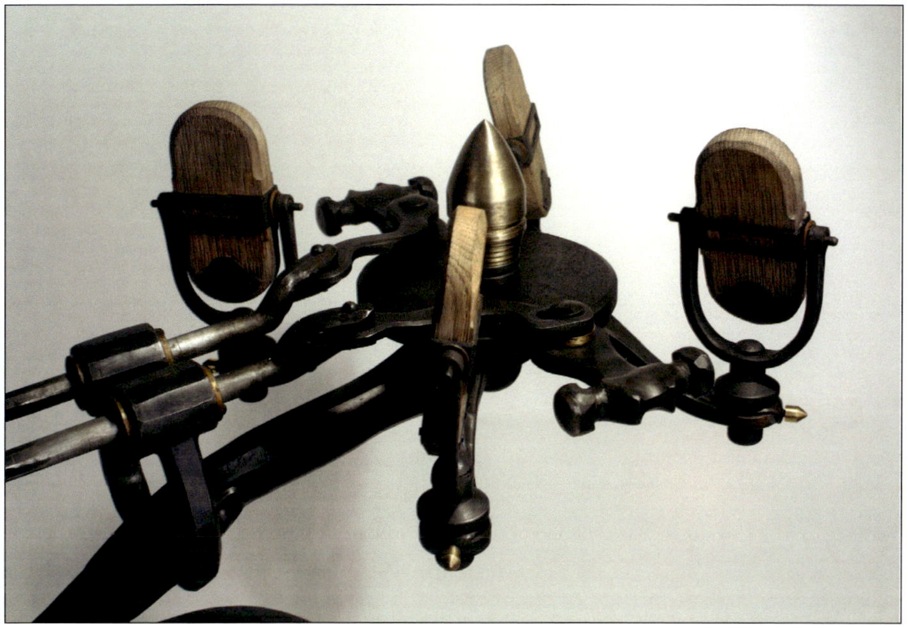

Michael Leo Chmielewski. *Confidential #3.* Forged, machined, and fabricated. Mild steel, coil spring, brass, and oak. 40″ x 36″ x 30″.

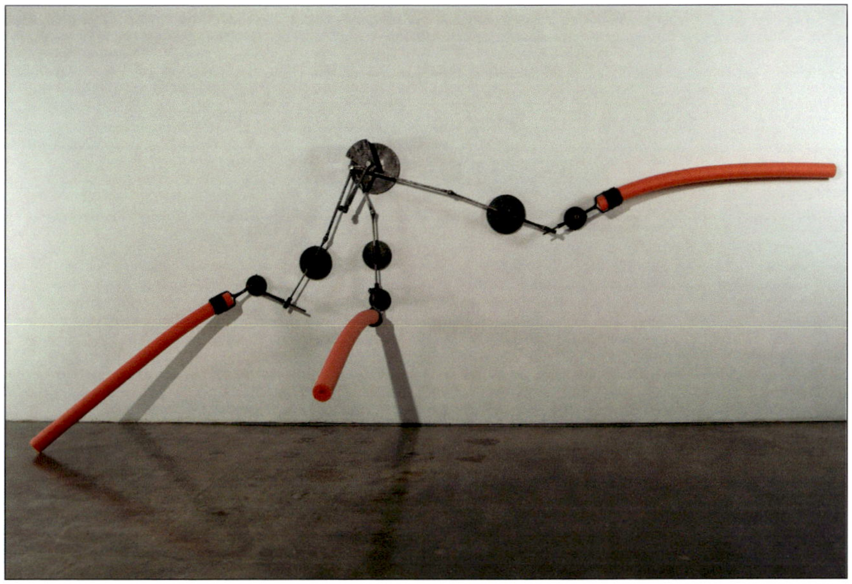

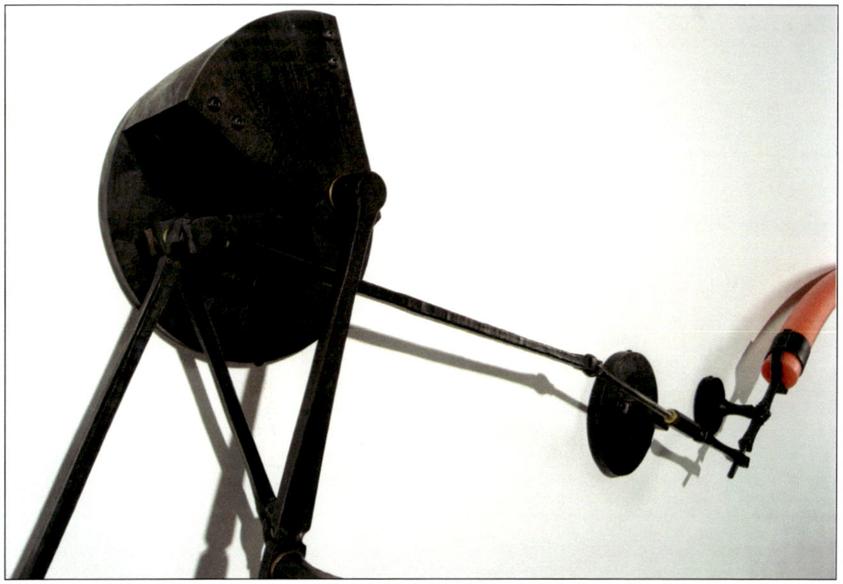

Michael Leo Chmielewski. *Configuration 2: Sweep, Dust, % ^ $&.* Forged, machined, fabricated. Mild steel, brass, polyethylene foam. 5′ x 18′ x 5′.

Shelly Cournoyer

Oakland, California, Shelly.Cournoyer@gmail.com

Artist's Statement

I create art in response to environmental, social, and philosophical issues with a focus on human-to-human interaction and human interaction with the environment. As a jeweler, blacksmith, and sculptor, metalsmithing is my primary means. I recontextualize found objects within my work, offering a point of departure for the viewer while creating a dialog between the finished sculptural form and the preconception of its parts. A portion of my work is created intuitively; the concept and form grows throughout the building process. Other times, my work is conceived and executed with a specific intent. I seek a balance between these approaches.

Individual Artwork

Seed Staff

Personal concerns regarding the changes occurring in the current world's way of producing food is what inspired this staff. The bulb element is a time capsule of tasty produce my community and I consumed. The branch protruding through the top of the glass bulb symbolizes determination and new growth for the generations to come.

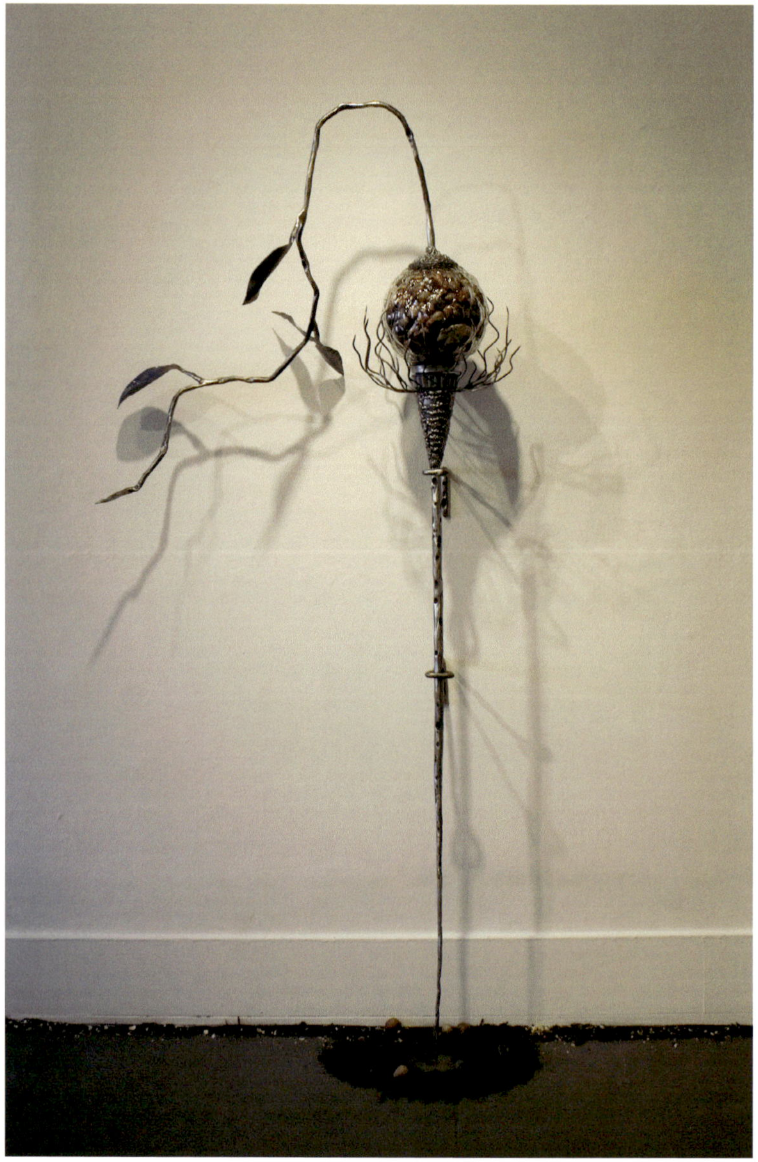

Shelly Cournoyer. *Seed Staff.* 2007. Steel, found glass, community collected seeds, nuts, and pits. 6′ 9″ h x 3′ 5″ w, 8″ x 10″ (bulb).

Venerable Tree

This tree was created thinking about a "holy" understanding for nature. Trees are more than necessary for human occupancy of this planet. However, every year there are tons of trees cut down for the development of malls and concrete jungles. This tree does not convert carbon monoxide into oxygen, but instead it stands as a symbol of an indestructible and sacred object for life.

Shelly Cournoyer. *Venerable Tree.* 2007. Steel. 8′ 9″ h x 19″ w at base x 4′ w at branches.

Bullet Tools

These garden bullet tools are part of a lager piece titled *Up-rooting Differences*. I have lived in several different areas of Oakland for the past eight years. In 2008/09, I finally lived in a house that had a yard to start a vegetable garden. It wasn't as easy as just buying plants and dropping them into the soil though. I started digging and began finding all sorts of old rubbish in the soil. So first I sifted the junk from the soil, then mixed in healthy organic soil, and finally planted my crops. I shared the produce my garden provided with my community and friends. Teaching others to garden and to care for both the earth and their bodies is more important than fighting and shooting one another.

Shelly Cournoyer. *Bullet Tools.* 2009. Steel, found bullet shells.
Trowel 1 1/2″ h x 5 1/2″ w x 9″ d. Fork 3 1/2″ h x 4 1/2″ w x 7″ d.

Double Leaf Buckle

I was interested in creating a newer version of my leaf belt buckle, this time with two leaves.

Gnarled Perch

This birdhouse was created and donated to a fundraiser promoting art activities, supplies, and classes. I decided to combine some of my collection favorites into a new treasure.

Shelly Cournoyer. *Double Leaf Buckle.* 2009. Steel. 2 1/4″ h x 3 1/2″ w x 1 1/8″ d.

Shelly Cournoyer. *Gnarled Perch.* 2009. Dodecagon structure, hardwoods, forged steel, and hollow formed copper. 21″ h x 7 1/2″ w x 7 1/2″ d.

Walking Bloom

Navigating through life is not easy, not for anyone. I travel on my own, occasionally sharing my path with another. Some friendships and intimate relationships are time sensitive, yet others will last a lifetime. *Walking Bloom* is a reminder for me to care for and to love many, but to always stay motivated by my own personal journey. Being able to see the beauty beyond the pain when in transitioning relationships, while also embodying the required strength to walk along, alone even, re-builds personal inner knowing. A walking staff implies and encourages forward motion.

Shelly Cournoyer. *Walking Bloom.* 2009. Steel, driftwood, hand-blown glass (glass blower: Evan Kolker). 76″ h x 11″ w x 9″ d.

Mike Edelman

Frostburg, Maryland, mike@medelmanart.com

Artist's Statement

Just like a writer uses words to express a complex idea in her or his head, in my sculptures, I try to convey an idea that transcends the medium, a feeling that I can express in no other way. Even in the furniture and functional work, a piece of my mind, a thought and an idea, a feeling, pass into the final product. In the end, the art simply becomes the tangible embodiment of an emotion.

Individual Artwork

Mike Edelman. Bench. Steel and black walnut. 58" x 49" x 24".

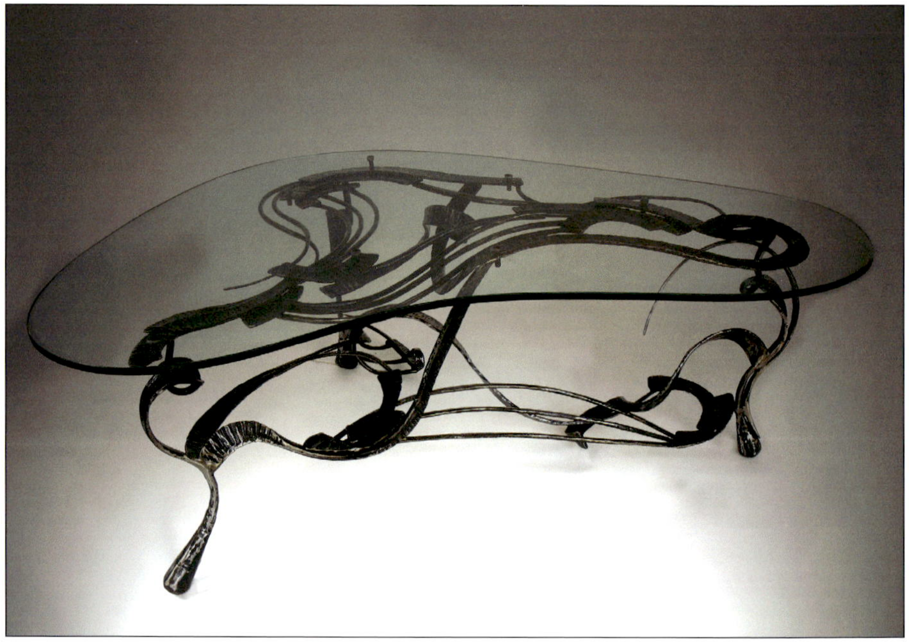

Mike Edelman. Coffee Table. Steel. 60" x 30" x 18".

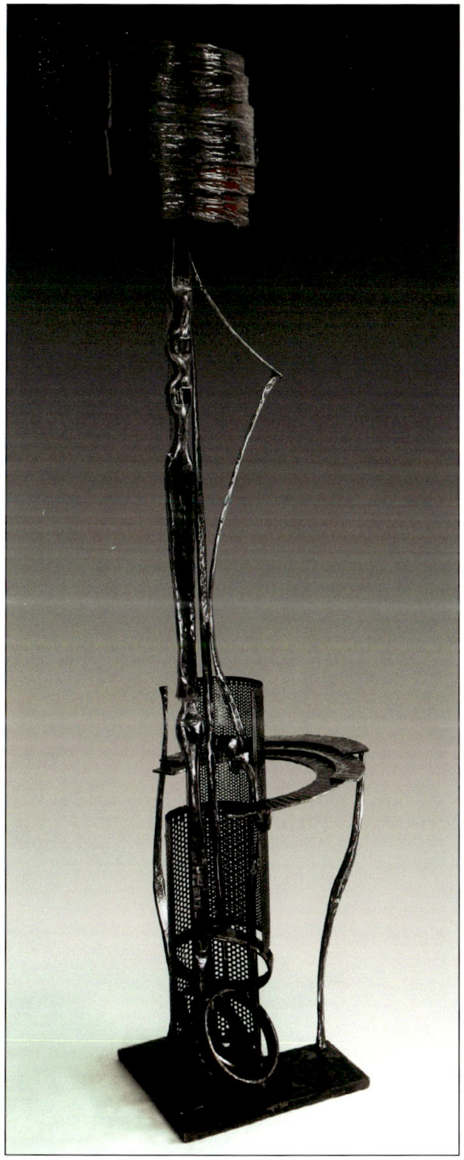

Mike Edelman. Entrance Light. Steel. 80″ x 18″ x 16″.

Mike Edelman. Wearable Sculpture. Forged brass and copper. 4″ x 5″ x 1″.

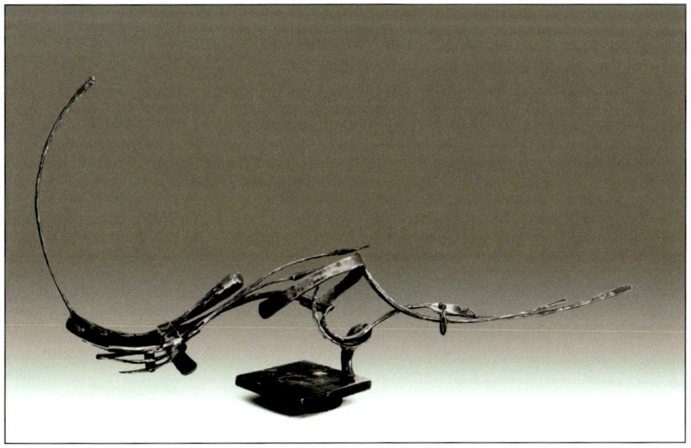

Mike Edelman. *Laying Woman*. Sculpture. Steel. 16″ x 30″ x 9″.

Mike Edelman. *Echo Series #1*. Sculpture. Steel with hardwood. 48″ x 20″ x 6″.

David Edwards

Emporia, Kansas, djedwards@cableone.net

Individual Artwork

Grape Vine Wreath

The grape motif of one of about a dozen botanical motifs I use in wreath construction.

David Edwards. Grape Vine Wreath. 2006. Forged and fabricated from mild steel with a natural black iron finish. 16" d. *Photo: J. Schrock Photography*

Rooster

The "O" form is a sculptural play on the Zen concept of Enso.

David Edwards. *Rooster*. Sculpture. 2006. Forged and fabricated mild steel table sculpture with brass brushed patina. 14" h. *Photo: J. Schrock Photography*

Cattail Motif Railing

Provides a botanical architectural accent to a newly constructed sunken courtyard garden with deck above.

David Edwards. Cattail Motif Railing. 2007. It is forged and fabricated from mild steel. *Photo: J. Schrock Photography*

Kansas Trees Book

The book "pages" are my way of recycling used band saw blade scrap by stacking and welding. The idea was inspired by recalling the Damascus billet building process.

David Edwards. *Kansas Trees Book*. Book table sculpture. 2007. Forging, chasing, repoussé, and hollow form fabrication techniques with mild steel. 1" x 4" x 6". *Photo: J. Schrock Photography*

Celtic Chess Set

The forged board pieces have rare earth magnets recessed in the bases for added stability. The two patinas are natural black iron and brass brushing. The board is the lid of the box that stores the pieces.

David Edwards. *Celtic Chess Set*. 2010. Forged and fabricated from heavy-duty mild steel. Table height: 24". Board pieces range from 5" to 8" h. *Photo: J. Schrock Photography*

Feathers

This collection of forged feather elements demonstrates slight variations in form. They can be incorporated into various rustic western Native American sculptural creations.

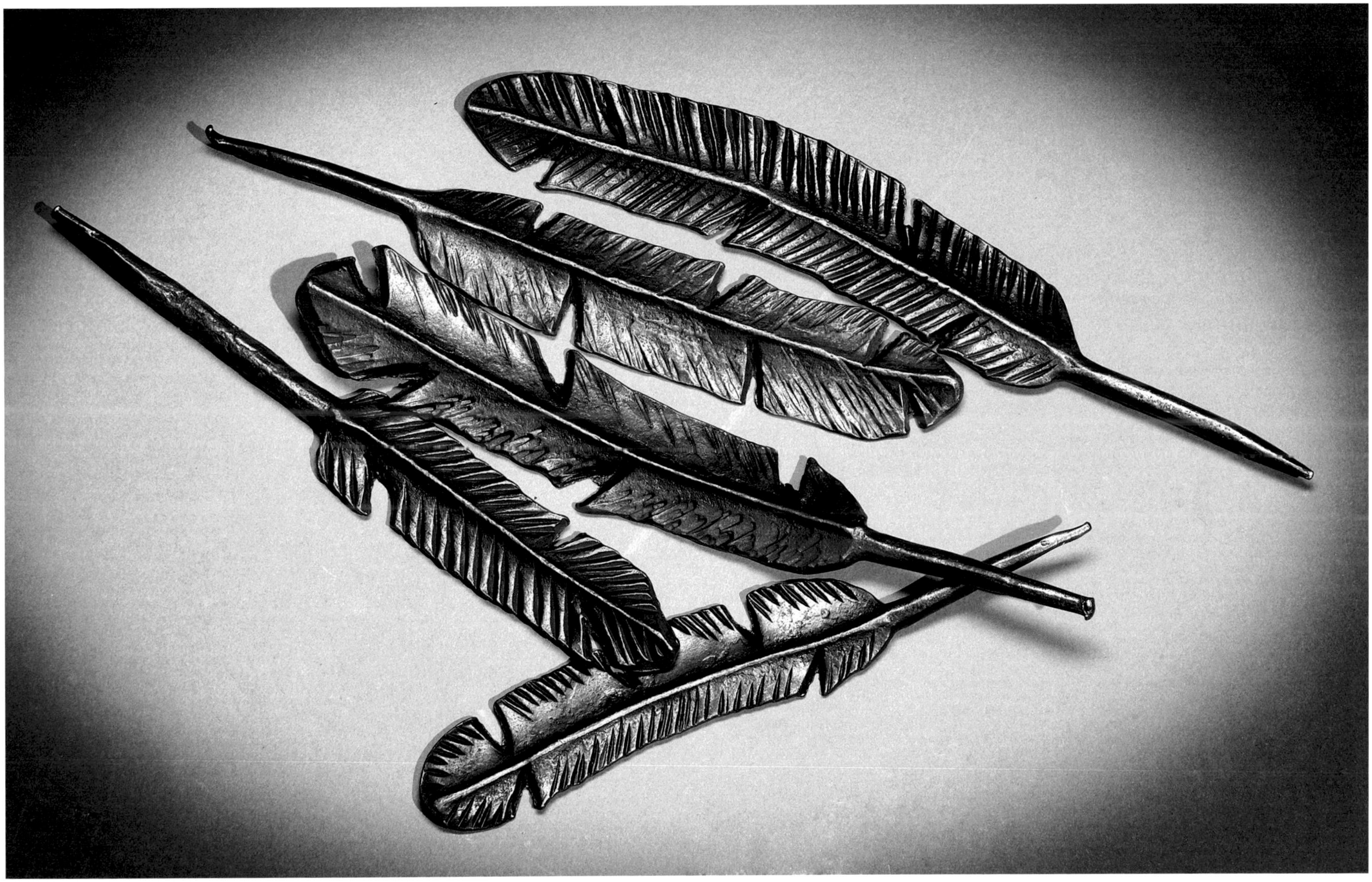

David Edwards. *Feathers.* 2008. Mild steel has been hot-chiseled, then finished in natural black iron. The feathers are about 8" long. *Photo: J. Schrock Photography*

Lisa Elias

Minneapolis, Minnesota, lisae@visi.com

Artist's Statement

As a metal artist, I am inspired by traditional blacksmithing techniques. I create elegant, functional sculptures. I draw on simple organic forms to fabricate my work. A linear fluid touch allows me to create a diversity of sculptures from fences, gates, and benches to light fixtures and arbors. The true power of my artistic ability is to harmonize the disparate elements of steel and gracefully turn them into organic sophisticated sculpture.

Individual Artwork

Tree Grate and Tree Corral

I designed, forged, and fabricated thirty of these artistic tree corrals and twenty bike racks for downtown Minneapolis during the summer of 2009. I worked closely with the city of Minneapolis to ensure everything was compliant with public safety. I am now building a functioning drinking fountain for the same area to reduce the purchase of plastic bottles and celebrate the city's great drinking water.

Lisa Elias. *Tree Grate and Tree Corral*. 2009. Corten steel. 48″ x 48″ x 40″ h. *Photos: Lisa Elias*

Patio Grille and Hanging Pendant Light

Lisa Elias. Patio Grille. 2009. Painted mild steel. 66″ w x 48″ h. *Photo: Lisa Elias*

Lisa Elias. Grille and Hanging Pendant Light. 2009. *Photo: Lisa Elias*

Entrance Gate and Panels

Lisa Elias. Entrance Gate and Panels, St. James Hotel Restaurant, Red Wing, Minnesota. 2010. Mild steel. 16′ x 8′ h. *Photo: Lisa Elias* (above and opposite page)

Lisa Elias. Side Panels, St. James Hotel. 2010. 4′ w x 8′ h.
Photo: Dan Marshall

Lisa Elias

Roberta Elliott

Cobden, Illinois, velhamer@midwest.net

Artist's Statement

My primary material is mild steel. I particularly enjoy using pipe. This hollow material gives an impression of mass without the actual weight and provides an additional surface (the interior) with its own potential to be worked. It is a form that requires a gentle and patient hammer blow to avoid collapsing it. Currently, I use only recycled pipe; the other ends are running around in John Deere tractors.

The versatility of mild steel allows it to take the bold shapes usually associated with ironwork, as well as the soft, feminine lines for which I strive. My work often contains botanical references, and I create images that evoke continuing growth. Each heat of the metal offers an opportunity to explore. The results can be unexpected, opening up an entirely new path leading to the spontaneity evident in many of my creations.

Then there is the fascination of forge welding. I am amazed every time I successfully perform this weld, in which two or more pieces are heated to 2600 degrees, carefully introduced to each other and firmly hammered into a single unit. Vigilance and focus are required; uncertainty and excitement are part of the process. I try to incorporate at least one forge weld in every piece I design. I use this process to introduce texture and images to the surface of my work.

Individual Artwork

Lahuna and Sunburst

For my vases, I use recycled pipe. When I heat it to around 2600 degrees Fahrenheit, I can forge weld various patterns onto it by simply hammering them into place. Depending on the size of the design, this may be in two heats or may take as many as twelve for each item.

Once I am sure the "garnish" is firmly attached, I forge the pipe into its vase shape. I neck down the top to fit a glass test tube so it can be used with fresh cut flowers. Next I neck down the bottom, separating off the section that will become the foot. Now comes tapering the midsection into its final shape. This involves collapsing the pipe into a tapered die I have specifically made for this purpose. I flare the top using a cross pein type die to ruffle it. I use a similar process to form the foot.

I soak the vase in vinegar for several days to dissolve the flux used in the forge welding stage. Depending on the complexity of the vase, I either wire brush or sand blast the vase to remove the remaining scale. When I heat the vase to a dull red and rub it with a brass brush, the brass bristles melt onto the vase, giving it a brass patina.

Roberta Elliott. *Lahuna.* Vessel. 2008. Forged steel pipe, rod, and fireplace curtain; abrasive brass patina. 18" x 8" x 4". *Photo: Larry Berman*

Roberta Elliott. *Sunburst.* Vessel. 2008. Forged steel pipe and angle iron: abrasive brass patina. 18" x 8" x 8". *Photo: Larry Berman*

Carnival!

In making my spoons, I push pipe in many directions. I forge out its center hole, split and taper one end, and flatten and drift a ring on the other end. For the "bowl," I forge weld-expanded steel or butterflies together or introduce playful human figures.

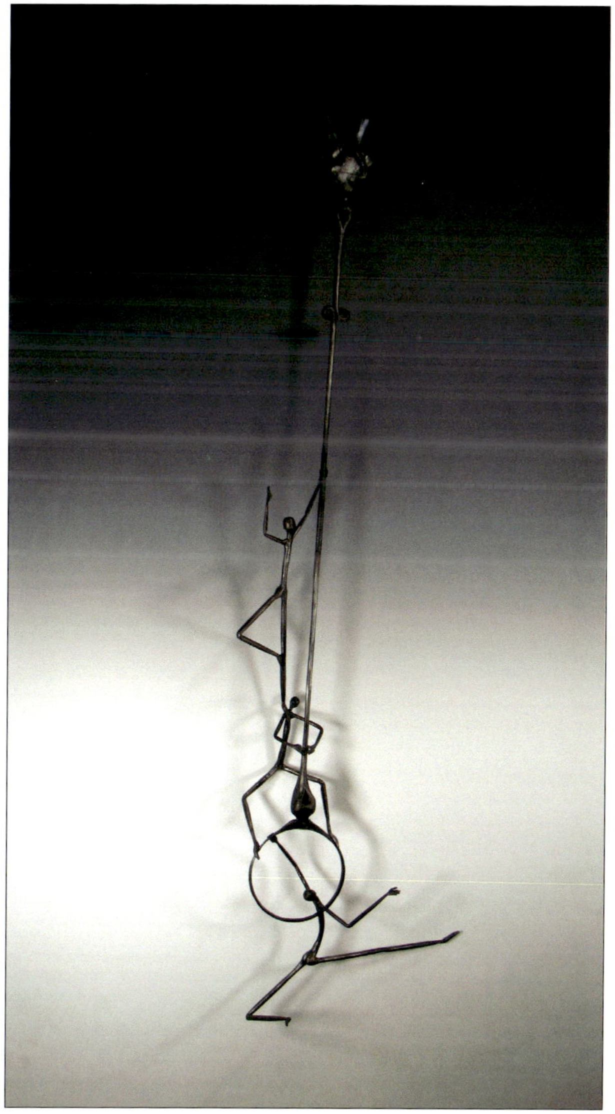

Roberta Elliott. *Carnival!* Dysfunctional Spoon. 2010. Forged steel pipe and rod. 24" x 6" x 4". *Photo: Roberta Elliott*

Champion Oak, Spring Splendor, and Weeping Willow

I first forge weld steel chips from a metal saw onto sheet to form a background of leaves. Next I hammer weld on a basic tree shape that I have cut out with a plasma cutter. Then I keep layering on more chips and various size wires for more leaves and branches. Tempering colors, brass patinas, and vegetable oil baked at a low temperature are the basis for the final patina.

Roberta Elliott. *Champion Oak.* Wall panel. 2010. Forged steel. 12" x 12" x 1". *Photo: Larry Berman*

Roberta Elliott. *Spring Splendor.* Wall panel. 2010. Forged steel. 12" x 12" x 1". *Photo: Larry Berman*

Roberta Elliott. *Weeping Willow.* Wall panel. 2010. Forged steel. 14" x 8" x 1". *Photo: Larry Berman*

Greg Eng

Formation Metal Arts, Vista, California, www.FormationMetalArts.com

Individual Artwork
Balcony Railing

Greg Eng. Balcony Railing. The corner posts are 1-inch solid steel. The scrolls and pickets are 1/2″ square bar forged to a round taper. The finish is blackened steel with a polyurethane clear coat. 38″ h x 8′ w. Private Residence in Del Mar, California. *Photo: Brenda Eng*

Staircase Handrail

Though the design is very simple, the execution was one of my more difficult stair projects. The spacing on each stair tread, the backing underneath each stair tread, positioning each picket vertically, having to space the knuckles from the top down, and not being able to cut the tops were all challenges. Lag bolts were used at the bottom of each picket as well as epoxy to lock the pickets in place. It would have been much easier to add a bottom rail to this design instead of the pickets going into the treads.

Greg Eng. Staircase Handrail. This forged handrail consists of 5/8" x 1 1/2" top cap with 5/8" forged and twisted pickets. The finish is patina steel, clear coated, and waxed. This handrail was built on site. Private Residence in Rancho Santa Fe, California. *Photo: Brenda Eng*

Vent Hood

To create a refined aged look, all surfaces have the effect of pitting and subtle distressing. The banding and half round details are brass; the panels are copper sheet laminated to a steel sub frame. The finish is burnished patina, sealed, and waxed. Special tools were made to create various styles of pitting and the old "beat it with a chain" technique (three styles of chain) worked well.

Greg Eng. Vent Hood. This vented hood is 32" h x 67" w x 25" d. Private Residence in Poway, California. *Photo: Brenda Eng*

Door Bell

This was the final item on a two-year project. The house had an old mission look and this was its fitting final piece of jewelry.

Greg Eng. Door Bell. This forged steel doorbell has riveting, tenons, bands, twisting, pressing, scrolling, and texturing—all manner of blacksmith work. Private Residence in Rancho Santa Fe, California. 54″ h x 15″ w. *Photo: Brenda Eng*

Gothic Gate

This pedestrian gate design was chosen from a source book featuring medieval ironwork. Special jigs were created to bend the triangle shaped stock.

Greg Eng. Gothic Gate. Solid steel outer frame 1 1/4″ bar, inner panel of 1/4″ sheet. Triangle shaped stock is riveted to 1/4″ sheet on both sides. The flat bar elements are forged and riveted to the inner frame. The finish is hot dipped galvanized, blackened, and sealed. Private Residence in La Jolla, California. 40″ x 71″. *Photo: Brenda Eng*

Loggia Entry Gate
Each square tenon was forged traditionally.

Greg Eng. Loggia Entry Gate. Forged steel. The bands attaching the 1/2" x 1" scrolls to the upper arched frame are fitted into indentations made in the 1" x 1 1/4" frame. The four inner horizontal bars are 5/8" x 1 1/4" and the four inner vertical bars are 1/2" x 1". All the components and frame were heavily textured to show up through the multiple layers of hot dipped galvanized, two-part marine epoxy and polyurethane topcoat. Piercing and forging to dimension were challenges for this project. Private Residence in Del Mar, California. 7'x 4'. *Photo: Brenda Eng*

Peg Fetter

St. Louis, Missouri, pegfetter@yahoo.com

Artist's Statement

My work is a combination of tough, gritty steel with the refined element of gold. I so appreciate the "wrongness" of this marriage. I have distilled my work down to the bare necessities, only creating what is necessary to convey my aesthetic.

Individual Artwork

Peg Fetter. *Wrap Rings*. 2002. Fabricated. Steel, 14kyg. 3/4" l x 3/4" h x 1/16" w each. *Photo: Don Casper*

Peg Fetter. *Stigmata Necklace* a.k.a. *Logan's Run Necklace.* 2006. Fabricated and forged steel, cast 14kyg, ruby. 16" l x 1" w x 1/4" d. *Photo: Don Casper*

Peg Fetter. *Nail Bracelet*. 2008. Fabricated. Forged steel, 14kyg.
7″ l x 1 1/4″ x 1/2″ h. *Photo: Don Casper*

Peg Fetter. *Snap Ring.* 2008. Fabricated steel, 14kyg, 3pt. diamond.
1 3/4″ l x 1/2″ w x 1 3/4″ h. *Photo: Don Casper*

Jeff Fetty

Spencer, West Virginia, jeff@jefffetty.com

Artist's Statement

The appeal of working with iron lies in the traditional role of blacksmiths in the community and the permanence of their work. Historically, blacksmiths contributed to the well-being of their neighbors by creating the tools that sustained the community. Their implements and art served and gave pleasure to many generations. In the same sense, my work allows me to share with a broader community of viewers, for which I am thankful. Hopefully, my art contributes to their well-being.

My growth as an artist requires looking along the timeline of my art. Through my travels, I have drawn from the sites of ancient metalworking, and the many European cities where the art form reached its zenith. My interaction with blacksmiths in this country and abroad shows me not only where the craft is today, but also where it will be tomorrow.

Nature is the greatest catalyst for my work, and, as I live in a rural setting, the natural world is intertwined with my existence. I am drawn to explore my setting through hiking, gathering, and photographing in the hills and hollows near my home. I am constantly searching for new shapes and forms to integrate into my work.

I hope to convey the essence of how I live and create, and to allow the viewer to experience the bonding of nature and art. In all of my creations, functional and sculptural, my goal is to fashion work that brings with it a moment of reflection and tranquility. Perhaps living close to the source as I do helps, but I, the artist, am merely an interpreter. Ultimately, it is the art form, the age-old craft of blacksmithing that works the magic.

Jeff Fetty. Bowl. 2007. Forged steel. 2" h x 6" w x 6" d. *Photo: Gefeti*

Individual Artwork

Bowl

I have created a series of forged bowls using recycled materials. This particular bowl is made from industrial grating repeatedly heated, folded, and hammered.

Console Table

This design was inspired by the French Art Deco work of Edgar Brandt. The design on the table apron is composed of individually, hand-forged steel with a bronze patina. The rectangle bands were forged from round stock to get both the size and look we wanted. The design on the bands is carved with customized hand-forged chisels made from automotive springs.

Jeff Fetty. Console Table. 2010. Forged steel with hand-rubbed wax finish and brass patina. Granite top. 30″ h x 60″ w x 18″ d. *Photo: Jim Osborn*

Fetty-Probst Table

This piece is a collaboration between Jeff Fetty and well-known furniture designer, Jim Probst. The table makes use of recent elements incorporated in their individual designs and is the first in a series of pieces that will reflect the creative spirit of their friendship.

Jeff Fetty. *Fetty-Probst Table*. 2009. Forged steel with cherry top. 30" h x 48" w x 18" d. *Photo: Jim Osborn*

Freshwater Bar

This commission for a nearby oil and gas developer utilized recycled pipe from his operations for the framing, foot rail, and lighting structure. The most intricate aspects of the piece are not obvious to the casual viewer. The framework required multi-directional supports to hold the tension created by the curve of the 3/8″ x 2 1/2″ upper steel band and 16 gauge steel skin. The brushed copper patina on the face of the bar was applied with a strong vertical accent to compliment other elements in the room. Lampshades are by West Virginia glass artist Ron Hinkle. Justin Burd, a young concrete artist, created the top with a flowing design of exposed aggregate that compliments the curve of the bar.

The working photo shows the bending of the foot rail from recycled 2″ gas pipe.

Jeff Fetty. *Freshwater Bar.* 2010. Forged steel with copper patina and decorative concrete top. 48″ h x 18′ w x 18″ d. *Photo: Gefeti*

Alan Flashing

Oakland, Oregon, flashing@centurytel.net

Artist's Statement

When I design I see the negative spaces as of equal importance as the positive ... it is a light and dark juxtaposition of being there and not, one without the other seems less.

Blacksmithing is a dance between the forge, the anvil, and the blacksmith. I believe that the modern blacksmith's work should depict his or her own time and look not to recreate the past, but rather to draw from it and craft our own work.

Individual Artwork

Winged Heart Walled Sconce

Alan Flashing. *Winged Heart Walled Sconce.* 2009. Forged and fabricated hollow form construction, cold chasing on the wing details with hot brass brushing for highlights. Plumbed for electrical wiring or may be set up as an oil lamp or candle. Mild steel. 12″ w x 16″ d x 9″.

Billiards Light

I called this light the "Nemo." It is what came to mind when I think of a billiards light on the Nautilus. The billiards light is paired up with an Arts and Crafts billiards table built in 1908.

Alan Flashing. *Billiards Light.* 2009. Forged and fabricated. Mild steel and copper. 33" h x 5' w x 16" d.

Balcony Railing

The panels have a symbolic meaning. The copper oval or egg sitting in the nest of Big Leaf Maple leaves represents home and family. The side panels were inspired by two motifs: one of *Yggdrasil,* the world tree in Norse mythology, and the other was a flowing river—flowing, as do our lives.

Alan Flashing. *Balcony Railing*. 2008. Forged and fabricated. Mild steel and copper. 40″ h; three 8′ panels; 24′ l (total). (right and opposite page)

Alan Flashing

Rebekah Frank

Joseph, Oregon, fraserironworks@gmail.com

Artist's Statement

Ostensibly, women have equal rights, but in the trenches of the everyday, my experiences proved otherwise. Art became the means to explore and understand issues of equality, power, struggle, and limitation. Artists such as Alberto Giacometti, Gina Pane, and Francesca Woodman inspire my work.

The awareness that I have gained throughout my professional career as a metal worker, I now apply to understanding the questions of gender normative behavior that are raised when people discover that I am a metalsmith, blacksmith, and machinist. Creating artwork with historically gendered processes and materials as a way to explore and analyze the constraints of gender lends conceptual underpinning and a layer of ironic humor to the work.

For me, concept, process, and material are inextricably connected.

Individual Artwork

Within

The surprise behind hidden doors, the wonder of containers, the power of gifts is explored in this piece. Behind a simple façade resides a whimsical play of materials and interactive motion. This piece invites the audience to engage with the piece, to uncover the unseen, and appreciate the hidden interior within.

Rebekah Frank. *Within.* Container. 2008. Machined steel, stainless steel cable, sterling silver, 50 Sky Blue Topaz. 8" d x 4" h. *Photos: Zachary Ferguson* (above and opposite page)

Extend

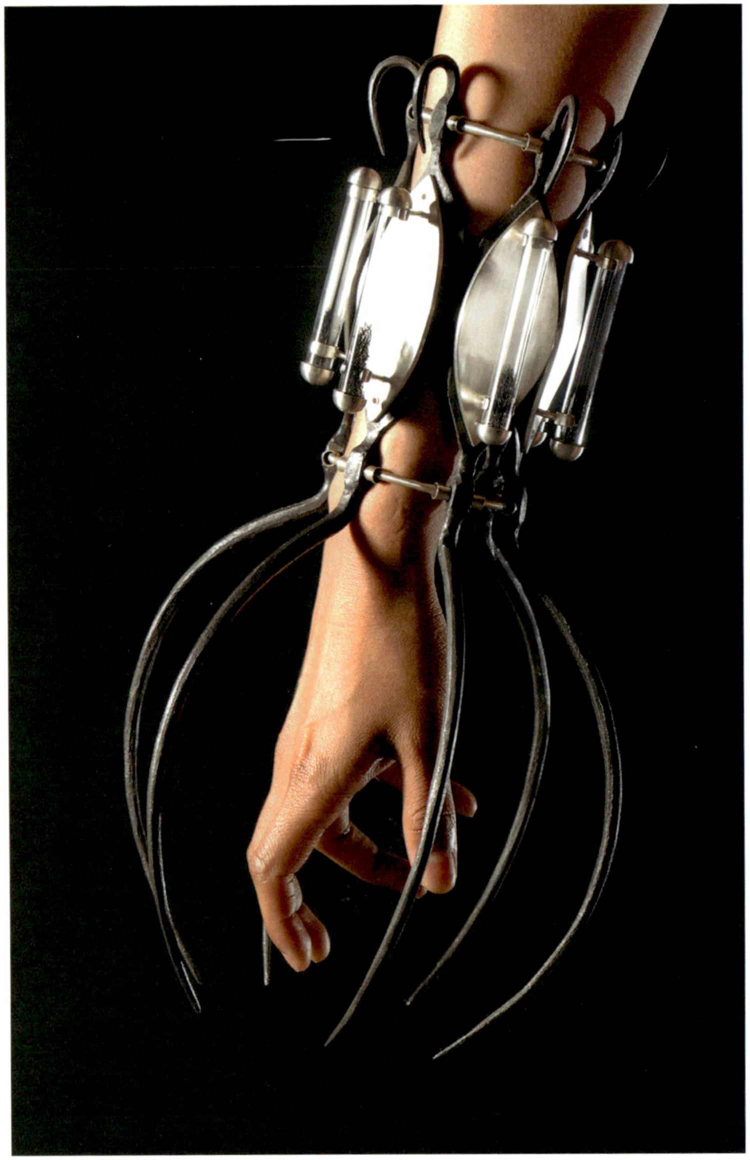

Rebekah Frank. *Extend.* Wearable Sculpture. 2009. Forged steel, fabricated sterling silver, glass, 2500 eyelash extensions. 16" x 8" in diameter at the widest, 4" in diameter at the wrist. *Photo: Zachary Ferguson*

Pinion

Rebekah Frank. *Pinion.* Wearable Sculpture. 2009. Forged steel, fabricated nickel silver. 20" l x 6" h x 4" d. *Photo: Zachary Ferguson* (above and opposite page)

Precarious

Here, the pieces act as pedestals for the human form, highlighting the extreme curve of the foot and flexion of the calf muscle. Exploring the limiting nature of modern high heels, this piece takes the lack of functionality to the extreme: the wearer is not able to stand. Lacking elements that attach the foot to the object, the foot must force itself into the curve without the benefit of the weight of the body or confining straps. There is an element of choice and desire in this piece, as there is in all fashion choices, yet it is the only one of my pieces that is actually uncomfortable to wear.

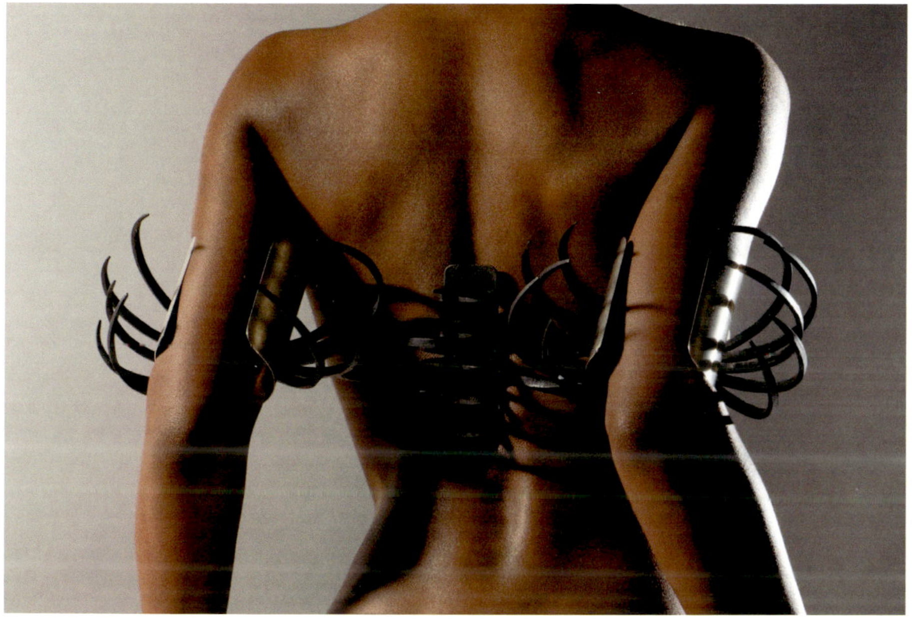

Rebekah Frank. *Precarious.* Wearable Sculpture. 2010. Forged and welded stainless steel. The pieces are 16" high and fit a size 8.5 women's foot. *Photo: Zachary Ferguson*

Chuck Fraser

Joseph, Oregon, fraserironworks@gmail.com

Individual Artwork

Chuck Fraser. Curved Stairs. Forged steel, reclaimed barn wood treads and risers. Calderas Restaurant, Joseph, Oregon.

Chuck Fraser. Pottery-shaped Gate. Forged steel, forged bronze roses (Eric Carlson, designer). 6′ x 8′. *HASSLACHER COLLECTION*.

Chuck Fraser. Entryway Arbor. Forged steel. 9′ x 4.5′.

Chuck Fraser. Calla Lilies. Forged steel. 24″ x 10″.

Chuck Fraser. Weather Vane. Forged steel, copper, hand blown glass. 5′ x 3′. *SHARON FORESTER COLLECTION*

Chuck Fraser. Hand Railing on Balcony. Forged steel (Eric Carlson, Designer). *HASSLACHER COLLECTION*

Mindy and Mark Gardner

Farmer City, Illinois, blacksmith@floodplainforge.com

Artists' Statements

Most of the ideas for my artwork come from nature—plants, animals or birds that I see while walking outdoors. Something as simple as a leaf as it dries and curls can be beautiful. I hope my nature-related artwork will cause viewers to pause and see the beauty of the world around them. I also use my work to make a statement about our world today.

I have always enjoyed drawing on paper and chasing seemed an excellent way to transfer my paper drawings to drawings on steel. By using a combination of chasing and repoussé, my work has a third dimension, similar to that of a relief woodcarving.

Mild steel lends itself very well to this type of work both due to its malleability and to the sharp detail I can achieve working with it.

Mindy Gardner

I have always been interested in blacksmithing. As a child I managed to burn up my parent's grill and sister's hair dryer trying to make a forge. When I was eleven my father bought me a forge and an anvil and turned me loose. Over the years I have learned a lot and now am very interested in using traditional joinery techniques in making contemporary work.

Mark Gardner

Individual Artwork

American Lotus Wall Hanging

The American Lotus wall hanging represents a beautiful plant native to North America. The techniques used to make the wall hanging are called chasing and repoussé. This involves working the metal from the front and back to give the design a third dimension, similar to a relief woodcarving. After the chasing and repoussé are finished, the work is hand-sanded, to remove the fire scale, and is ready to color. For that I leave the areas that are white, such as the flower, as bare steel. The leaves and stems are brass colored, the color created by using a brass wire brush and heat. The dark background is gun bluing. The finish is oil and Renaissance Wax. (opposite page)

Mindy Gardner. *American Lotus*. Wall Hanging. 2008. Chasing. 12 gauge mild steel. 19″ h x 13″ w 1/2″ depth. *Photo: Mark Gardner*

Apple Blossoms Wall Hanging

The coloring on this piece is done using the bare metal for the white flowers and a brass brush and torch to transfer the brass coloring to leaves and the stems. The background is gun bluing. The "mat" that the artwork is riveted to is sandblasted and then blued, leaving a blue finish that is not as shiny as the finish surrounding the flowers.

Mindy Gardner. *Apple Blossoms.* Wall Hanging. 2008. Chasing and repoussé. The finish is oil and Renaissance Wax. 14 gauge mild steel with a16 gauge mild steel "mat." 23 3/4" h x 12" w x 1/2" depth. *Photo: Mark Gardner*

Shells by the Seashore End Table

The Shells by the Seashore end table is a combined effort by Mark and Mindy. The tabletop, created by Mindy, is made of three pieces of 12 gauge mild steel. The first piece of steel had two shells chased and repousséd on it, which represents the beach. The second piece of steel, which is colored blue by using Baroque Art Guilders Paste, represents the water. The third piece of steel has a wave design chased into the metal and represents the sea. The blue part of the table is lower than the metal on either side of it. Mark accomplished this by milling out part of the base to which the tabletop is riveted.

The table base, made by Mark, is hand forged and assembled using traditional joinery methods. The entire table was hand sanded to remove the fire scale and finished with oil and Renaissance Wax.

Mark and Mindy Gardner. *Shells by the Seashore.* Small End Table. 2009. Chasing and repoussé. 25" h x 20" w x 21" l. *Photo: Doug Carr. Photo is the property of the Illinois State Museum and the Illinois Artisans Program*

John W. Gehl

Manitowish Waters, Wisconsin

Individual Artwork

Ascending

The graceful upward sweep of the copper and the gentle rotation of the scroll create the feeling of exhilarating entry into space—a feeling of joy and excitement.

John W. Gehl. *Ascending.* Polished copper and forged steel. 24″ h x 8″ x 14″. *Photo: Doug Bailey*

Calla Lilies

John W. Gehl. *Calla Lilies*. Forged, riveted, and welded steel. Beeswax and linseed oil coating. 48″ h x 24″ x 24″. *Photo: John Jagodzinski*

Coat Rack

This sturdy coat rack is reminiscent of work found in old German homes and inns.

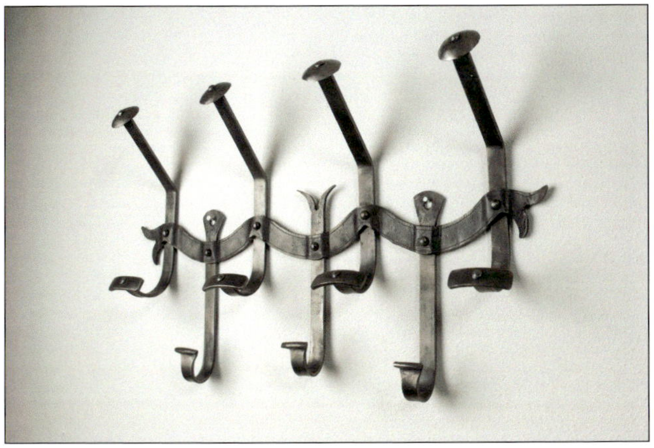

John W. Gehl. Coat Rack. Forged steel, acrylic clear seal. 36″ l x 12″ h x 8″. *Photo: John Jagodzinski*

Coneflower

John W. Gehl. *Coneflowers.* Forged and folded steel, flame colored, brass brush finish, acrylic coating. 16″ h x 12″ x 14″. *Photo: Doug Bailey*

Railing

The handrail is forged from heavy square stock to provide both a pleasant feel and a comfortable grip. The mono-post design is angled towards the user, while moving the base out of the way. The decorative sunflower motif is bolted to the base so that it can easily be changed with the seasons or styles.

John W. Gehl. Railing. Forged, welded steel. The railing is powder coated, the decorative flowers are flame colored and clear coated. 65″ h x 48″ l x 24″ d. *Photo: Doug Bailey*

Tsunami

The fury of a tsunami, and the arched beauty of the waves combine to create visual interest, and a visceral feel of the sea.

John W. Gehl. *Tsunami.* Forged steel, flame colored, gun bluing, Beeswax coating. 12″ h x 10″ x 10″. *Photo: Doug Bailey*

Greg Gehner

Edinboro, Pennsylvania, ggehner@transitforge.com

Artist's Statement

A major focus of my aesthetic is on the interplay between line and mass. Often the mass is concentrated at connections or realized through joinery, which emphasizes both the line/mass contrast and the assembly process. Designs are strongly influenced by industrial, agricultural, and architectural elements, as well as themes of motion, stasis, and equilibrium.

Individual Artwork

BLOCKY Candlestick

Mass was the main focus of this double candlestick. I like direct function with obvious connections, to show a blend of modern and traditional. Growing up on a farm with large post and beam barns I feel that my aesthetic often refers back to that type of straightforward wooden construction.

Greg Gehner. *BLOCKY Candlestick*. 2006. Forged. Steel. 6" x 7" x 8". *Photo: artist*

SOLID & MANIFOLD Tables

These pieces began with the tops, which I found at a local scrap yard. Sometimes I will adapt a design to utilize an interesting piece of material that I modify to suit the end form and purpose. The perforated circle was cleaned up and patinated, but was mostly unchanged for the *Manifold Table*, yet with the *Solid Table* I cut and shaped the large, industrial c-channel. In both cases, I emphasized prominent connections as design features.

Greg Gehner. *SOLID Table.* 2009. Forged and fabricated, with gun blue patina. Steel, salvaged metal. 18″ x 18″ x 22″. *Photo: artist*

Greg Gehner. *MANIFOLD Table.* 2009. Forged and fabricated, with gun blue and ferric chloride/ferric nitrate patina. Steel, salvaged metal. 18″ x 18″ x 22″. *Photo: artist*

GG200 Fire Tool Set

Riveted steel truss bridges inspired the look of this fire tool set. From bold rivets and the flat steel cross members, this set follows the same uncomplicated functionality.

Greg Gehner. *GG200 Fire Tool Set*. 2006. Forged and fabricated. Steel. 26″ (tools) / 30″ x 8″ x 12″ (overall). *Photo: artist*

***STRUT* Floor Lamp**

I wanted this floor lamp to have motion as a sculptural piece. A morphing repetition (in the legs) suggests it might be walking.

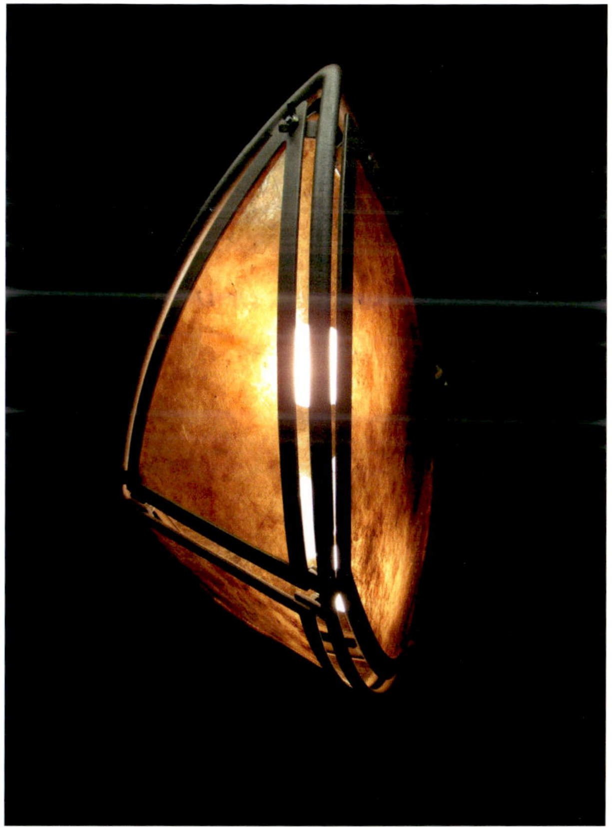

Greg Gehner. *STRUT.* Floor Lamp. 2010. Cold press and roll formed, fabricated, with ferric chloride/ferric nitrate patina. Steel, mica. 30" x 36" x 72". *Photo: artist*

Jennifer Gilbert

Las Vegas, Nevada, urbanIron@gmail.com

Artist's Statement

I make things that have a practical everyday purpose. My beds are for sleeping on, my door hardware opens and closes doors, my urns hold remains, and my lamps light the dark. Yet, I am making a statement about the human condition with my work. I am creating furnishings that I expect to last for generations, rather than be immediately disposable like most of today's wares. I am creating furnishings that I expect to prod people out of their visual complacency. My work must be noticed. It must be seen. I expect my work to force people to reassess their environment, see the branches and the leaves as if for the first time, and see the doorknob when they enter the room. I expect people to touch, to fondle, to caress, and ultimately, to posses my work.

I will continue to expand the conversation about what everyday objects should be—not overlooked but embraced.

Individual Artwork

Glass and Steel Passage Set

Fully functional door passage set: The mounting plates were forged from 2" x 1/4" steel flat bar. Larry Domsky of Domsky Glass made the blown glass knob. I made this set as an indoor passage set for a dark wood door. The other side of the door used a different glass piece for the knob. This, along with the faux keyhole cover, was added for visual interest.

Jennifer Gilbert. *Glass and Steel Passage Set.* 2009. Forged steel and glass. 8" x 3" x 2 1/4" and 8" x 2 1/2" x 2 1/2" opposite side.

Steel Passage Set

Fully functional forged steel indoor passage set: The mounting plate was forged from 2 1/2″ x 3/16″ flat bar and the knob was forged from 3 1/2′ dia. x 1/8″ discs. This set was made for an unpainted interior door.

Brushed Steel Door Pull

This piece was forged from three pieces of 1 1/4″ x 1/4″ flat bar for the mounting plate. The pull was forged from 1/2″ square bar and the pivot from 1″ round solid. I made two pulls total as an entry set for a double door entry.

Jennifer Gilbert. *Forged Steel Door Passage Set.* 2009. Forged steel. 11 1/2″ x 3 1/4″ x 3 1/2″ and 11 1/2″ x 3″ x 3″.

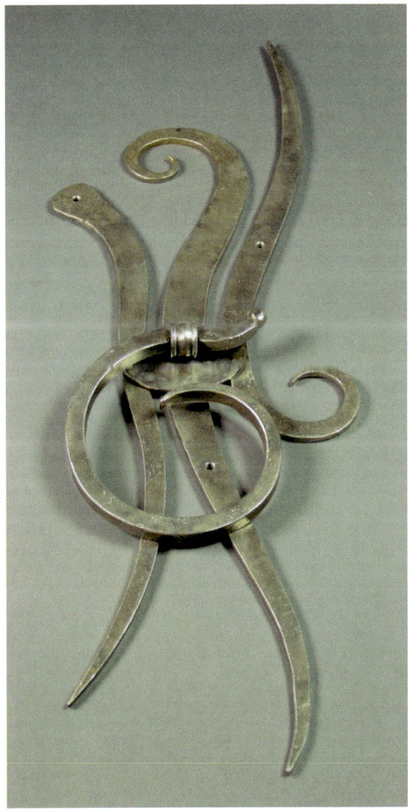

Jennifer Gilbert. *Brushed Steel Door Pull*. 2010. Forged steel. 27″ x 9″ x 1 1/2″.

Joshua A. Goss

Carbondale, Illinois, Joshua.goss@hotmail.com

Artist's Statement

Topography is subject to pressure; terrain is altered through friction and heat over time. Geological environments are forged, expending stored energy, exposing the fundamental nature of earth's development. Through the layering, welding, forming, and etching of iron and steel, geological transformations are simulated in my sculpture.

The *Shell Form Series* is representative of fossil materials. As vestiges of evolution, they have been stretched and eroded in metamorphosis and deposition. The *Structural Series* is characterized by the uplift and faulting that originates from the collision of tectonic plates. As mountains rise, fractures and folds expand through the earth's crust. With exposure to the atmosphere, organic textures are etched into underlying structures and patterns are revealed.

Theories of earth's development are based on hypothesis and objective observation. Erosion and deformation reveal the plasticity of substances often considered unyielding. The investigation of elementary materials, pliable and transferable, informs my understanding of the earth and processes within.

Individual Artwork

Joshua A. Goss. *Shell Form 5.* 2009. Steel, paint, ferric nitrate. Patina. 22" x 18" x 24". *Photo: Sun Kyoung Kim*

Joshua A. Goss. *Shell Form 7*. 2009. Steel, ferric nitrate. Patina. 20″ x 10″ x 15″. *Photos: Sun Kyoung Kim*

Joshua A. Goss. *Shell Form 14*. 2010. Iron, steel, wall mounted. 108" x 24" x 20".
Photo: Sarah Renshaw

Joshua A. Goss

Joshua A. Goss. *Structural 1 (Thrust).* 2011. Iron, steel. 18″ x 7″ x 9″. *Photo: artist*

Joshua A. Goss. *Structural 2 (Horst und Graben).* 2011. Iron, steel. 24″ x 10″ x 8″. *Photo: artist*

Joshua A. Goss

Seth E.H. Gould

Harwich, Massachusetts, sgould@meca.edu

Process and Techniques

Carving Set—This carving set was created with the ideas of tradition and heirloom objects in mind. The scrollwork that makes up the handles was forged as individual pieces and then welded together with a mini-torch. The ivory was cut, carved, and polished to fit by hand.

Joinery Study No.2, Joinery Study No.3—Understanding construction can give insight to many aspects of an object, not only how it was made, but also the maker's preference of tools and methods. This can often lead to a better understanding about the maker, time in which it was built, or concept behind the piece. Construction and technique are aspects of making that all makers must be versed in to accurately execute any project. These pieces are an exploration in construction using traditional joinery techniques to create rather abstract objects that inherently reference utility.

Saw—This saw was made after seeing a similar saw at the 2010 ABANA conference. Making this saw was an introduction to whitesmithing. It opened many doors by allowing me to start to understand another facet of iron. Each piece was forged and then refined and detailed with files and abrasives.

Individual Artwork

Seth E.H. Gould. Carving Set. 2008. Steel, ivory. 11.5″ x 3.5″ x 1″.
Photo: Robert Diamante

Seth E.H. Gould. Joinery Study No. 2. 2009. Steel. 22″ x 27″ x 7″.
Photo: Robert Diamante

Seth E.H. Gould. Joinery Study No. 3. 2009. Steel. 14″ x 14″ x 15″.
Photo: Robert Diamante

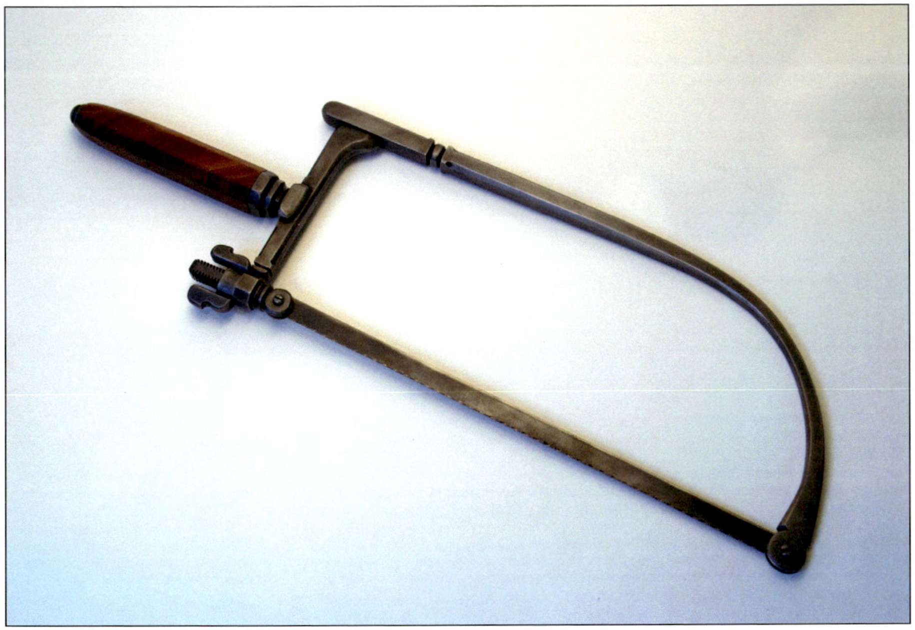

Seth E.H. Gould. Saw. 2010. Steel, mahogany. 18″ x 5.5″ x 1″.
Photo: Seth Gould

Grizzly Iron, Inc., Rodger and Jason La Brash

Phoenix, Arizona

Individual Artwork

Forged Vessel

Wrought iron forged from square bars salvaged from cutoffs of an antique gate that was made into an entry door for a restaurant.

Grizzly Iron, Inc. *Forged Vessel*. 2008. Forged. Wrought iron. Beeswax finish. 11″ x 11″ x 3″. *Photo: Tim Harper*

Passion Flower

Grizzly Iron, Inc. Rodger "Grizz" LaBrash. *Passion Flower*. 2009. Forged and fabricated. Steel. 60″ x 60″ x 30″. *Photo: Tim Harper*

Ottomans

These ottomans were made for a client's bedroom, taking inspiration from their existing bedroom furniture. The existing furniture is made from carved wood, so making the ottomans was a bit of a challenge. The ottomans are made from solid square bar.

Grizzly Iron, Inc. Ottomans. 2010. Forged and fabricated. Steel. 28" x 19" x 19".
Photo: Tim Harper

Driveway Gates

The driveway gates have elk forged from plate, taking inspiration from the many deer and elk mounts within the home.

Grizzly Iron, Inc. Driveway Gates. 2010. Forged and fabricated. Steel. 14' x 4'.
Photo: Jason LaBrash

Jorgen Harle, Jeff Holtby, and Jake James

Jorgen Harle: Eastsound, Washington, www.jorgenharleblacksmith.com;
Jeff Holtby: Langley, Washington, jeffholtby@Whidbey.com;
Jake James: Sooke, British Columbia

Artists' Statements

Since 2007, artist blacksmiths Jorgen Harle, Jeff Holtby, and Jake James have joined talents, facilities, and forges to co-produce large public and private commissions. As a new northwest collaborative, they meld a wide range of styles, influences, and shop capabilities. Their collaboration allows them to produce large commissions in a very short time without compromising the quality of their work.

Individual Artwork

Gate

These three accomplished smiths banded together for an epic two weeks of twelve-hour days to produce this seven-foot tall, 800-pound, heroically forged steel gate. *Gate* was their first true collaboration from inception to finish. The design shows a clear break with traditional concepts in gate composition. It focuses on the hinge detail and develops outward from there, dispensing with the notion of a frame and relying on the mass of the material used to provide the structural support for the gate.

The gate was forged from four- and three-by-one inch flat bar; they used exaggerated punching and pass-through joinery and heavy texture to capture the movement and life that is so evident in hot steel during the forging process. (opposite page)

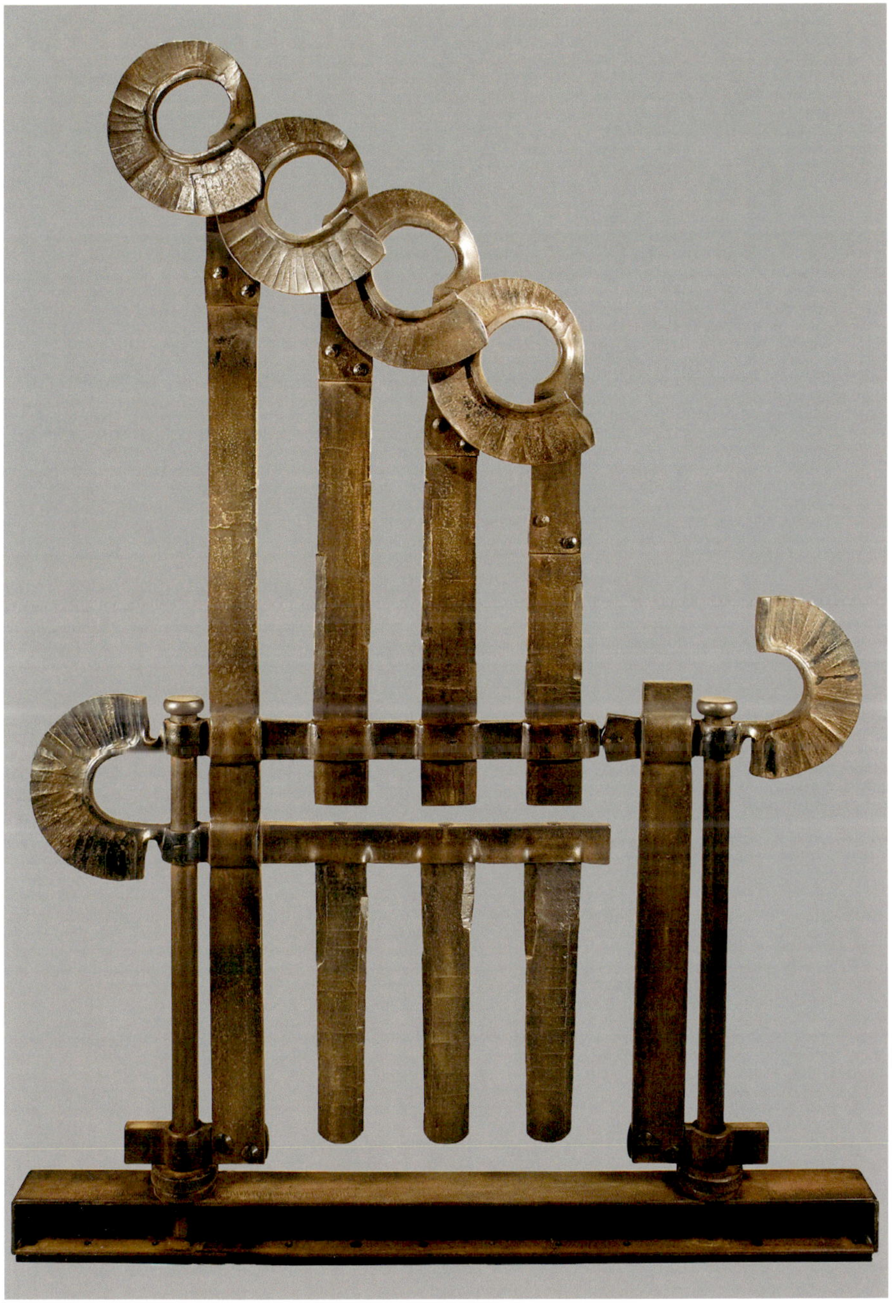

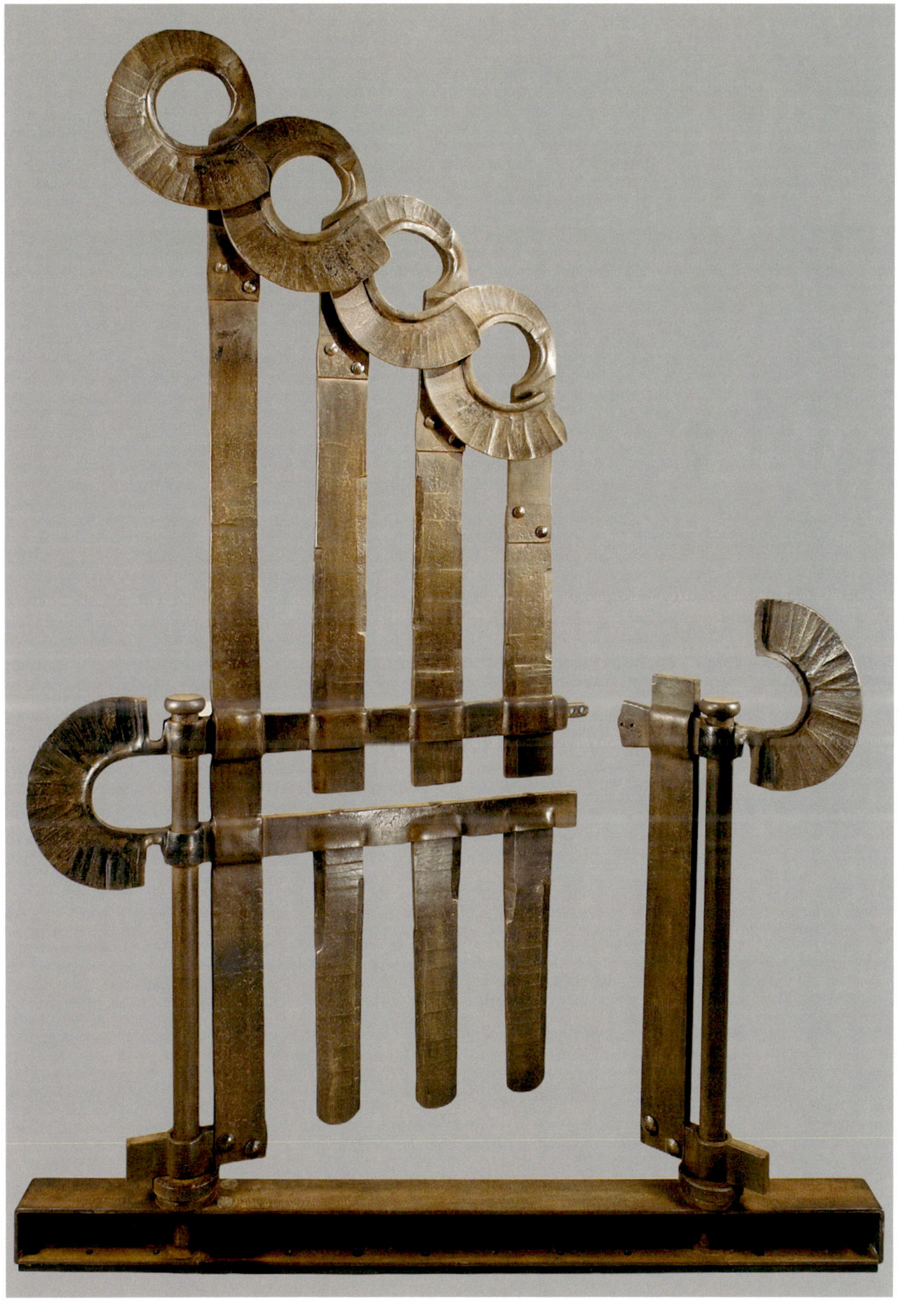

Jorgen Harle, Jeff Holtby, and Jake James. *Gate.* 2010. Using traditional joinery to express a contemporary form. Both sides of the gate pivot on two, vertical, inch-and-a-half round bars passing through slit and drifted journals. Steel gate is seven feet tall, five feet wide, and weighs 800 pounds. Verticals forged from 1″ x 4″ stock, horizontals from 1″ x 3″ stock. *Photo: Bill Ruth: ©2010bill@billruth.com*

Helmut Hillenkamp

Santa Fe, New Mexico, Helmut@iron-to-live-with.com

Artist's Statement

Sometimes there is not much to be said about new work, other than that it is done in a spirit of exploration and following my own desires.

Individual Artwork

Cowry Shell

Cowry Shell was a sculpture made for my Capoeira teacher, Pete Jackson, who uses the cowry shell motif in the logo of his school. It took about seventy hours to weld. I don't know the weight, but it turned out to be really heavy to move, even with the help of several strong guys.

Helmut Hillenkamp. Cowry Shell. Sculpture. Forged pipe scraps (left over from a railing job). Approximately 4' l. Photos: artist

Dr. Seuss-ish Fence

Rebar and wrought iron have always been my favorite materials, maybe because they are so basic. In this piece I combined them with each other to make a free flowing fence around a house.

Helmut Hillenkamp. Dr. Seuss-ish Fence. Rebar, wrought iron. Photos: Maria de las Casas.

Dietrich Hoecht

Clayton, Georgia, potsniron@windstream.net

Individual Artwork

Candles Sconces

These two 24″ long candle sconces are forged from angle iron, which is first flattened and then stretch hammered alternately at the sides. The follow-on twisting and bending of the pieces is inspired by the leaf shapes of a flowering cactus. Pyrite crystals are affixed behind the candle to reflect the flame in sparkles.

Dietrich Hoecht. *Candles Sconces*. Forged. Angle iron. Each 24″ l.

Dresser

This bathroom furniture piece was sized by using the last available slab of spalted pecan cut from a large diameter pecan log. The individual storage compartments are fronted with smaller pieces of pecan and white oak. The knob holds are found pine knots.

Instead of traditional slide installation drawers, this dresser's compartments are made to pivot forward for access. The center column is created by fullering an iron pipe at intervals. Mounting support brackets are affixed by tightening their forged spike ends like twist ties at the necked-down zones of the post. Compartment fittings are forged copper and colored with brown copper ferrite patina. The two vertical pivot rods are gray patinated bronze. In order to prevent the fully loaded boxes from pivoting forward all at once and making the dresser tip, a wall anchor is used to stabilize it.

Dietrich Hoecht. Dresser. 30″ h x 30″ w x 16″ d.

Bird of Paradise Gate

This gate is used to exclude children and dogs from a room, while keeping the wooden door open. Cats may squeeze by the lower gap toward the doorframe. The arrangement of forged iron elements is made to conform to building code spacing requirements. A lever/latch combination is pre-loaded with a leaf spring and permits snap engagement with the door post fitting (not shown) and allows gate rotation and locking from both directions. The diagonal member serves to structurally strengthen the gate against sagging forces, just as practiced traditionally with barn doors and their diagonally set boards.

Dietrich Hoecht. *Bird of Paradise Gate*. Hammered, repousséd, chased, welded. Steel sheet metal. Torch enameling color (carefully mixed and spread enamel powder avoided a gaudy color overload). Gate size: 29″ w x 36″ h.

Jeff Holtby

Langley, Washington, jeffholtby@Whidbey.com

Artist's Statement

The forging process is mesmerizing. I love hot metal, the way I can shape it to my will even though it seems indestructible. I put heat and steel together with my power hammer, a nimble giant waiting to be told what to do. It's a highly choreographed dance: I have to keep up with it at 180 blows a minute, and must make my moves when the material is at just the right temperature. I'm drawn by the fluidity of the process and find it compelling and absorbing.

Blacksmithing works with the most transformative material: it is hard, enduring, and obstinate until briefly softened to clay's malleability, at which time I make what I want, and then let it re-harden. There is an air of mystery about the results: to see bars pass through bars, hard steel bent into a knot, hard-edged metal wrought to form soft-edged organic figures. I find it magical to form something seemingly tenacious and unyielding into useful and ornamental objects that convey warmth, endurance, and continuity.

Blacksmithing carries with it a community heritage and through it I can produce handmade work that creates a warm and welcoming environment. I am able to create a personal and friendly touch, a sense of the hand-done that is enduring, and, I believe, promotes a feeling of permanence and community.

Jeff Holtby of Arcane Metal Arts. Freestanding pinecone fireplace screen and tools. Hand-forged tri-fold steel screen stands 5′ x 3 1/2′. *Photo: Bill Ruth: ©2010bill@billruth.com* (above and opposite page)

Individual Artwork

Pinecone Fireplace Screen

The fun thing about working in the Pacific Northwest is not being tied to any particular style and I like everything from traditional to contemporary to representational. I'm often called upon to represent typical Pacific Northwest flora and fauna. In this case, the customer wanted to represent the native trees on the bluff in front of his home. The pinecones were shaped in a die leaving the mass for the cone and a tapered stem defined. The petals were carved in hot, with a hand chisel. The pine needles were fifty feet of wire hammered into a triangular die so it would look needle-like. The lengths of wire were then cut, folded in half, bunched together in clusters, stuffed into small tubing, and then forge-welded together. The fireplace screen was assembled by riveting a screen between an inner and outer frame with offset corner joints to keep everything in the same plane.

Round Door and Lock Mechanism

A client contracted me to construct a round door with ornate hinges, a knob in the center, and a complex locking mechanism for a children's playhouse on his property. I engaged two woodworkers, Bruce Schwager and John Shinneman, as well as blacksmith Jorgen Harle to assist with the hot work. A round door presents a number of challenges because the hinges need to be unusually close together and therefore extremely stout and well anchored to both jam and door. The door was constructed with a steel armature inside that picked up the hinges and wood and left a chase from the striker to the center of the door to accommodate the latch work. The lock work was designed so that the knob on the outside and the knob on the inside moved independently from each other; the latch could always retract and the outside doorknob could be locked without affecting the inside knob. The owner wanted security but didn't want his children locked inside. The lock work required the three processes of forging, fabrication, and machining.

Jeff Holtby of Arcane Metal Arts. Round Door. 2009. Hinges were hot forged and lock and latch assemblies were forged, fabricated, and machined. Steel, wood, and bronze. Door diameter is four and a half feet. Hot work assistance by Jorgen Harle of Orcas Island Forge and woodwork by Bruce Schwager and John Shinneman. *Photo and latch work design: Jeff Holtby.*

Daniel Hopper

Oakland, California, daniel@danielhopper.com

Artist's Statement

My goal is to use metal to help bring a space to life. I want the viewer to be inspired to describe my work with adjectives not nouns—strong, quiet, dramatic, as opposed to railing, chandelier, chair. I design metal to activate and participate in the space it occupies. Using patterns and design concepts found in nature, I allow the metal forms to become their own being, rather than force them to strictly represent or imitate nature.

My work can be viewed as functional art. I have found no reason to separate architecture from sculpture, furniture from art, the visual from the tactile. I seek to create interactive, functional, architectural pieces that people feel compelled to touch, objects that are simultaneously whimsical and ominous.

Individual Artwork

BBQs

This design transpired from the client's openness to me blending art with function. He wanted two BBQs and he liked Venus flytraps. I thought that an organic, industrial approach would help accent the aggressive characteristics of the plant. I also created two pitcher plant tiki torches and a third pitcher plant to hold the cooking utensils. These two BBQs were created for a residence in San Francisco. The client wanted one to cook meat on and another for vegetables. I bought a used Webber grill from Craigslist, to alter and use as a form for the grill basin and lid. I then heated sheet metal, wrapped it over the form, and riveted it into place. The cilia are tapered tube and solid steel, which act as utensil hangers while you're cooking. Large diameter tube was forged, cut up, and stitch welded over a structural frame. The welds were left untouched to add to the organic/industrial BBQ concept.

Daniel Hopper. *BBQs.* 2005. Steel and stainless. 21″ x 33″ x 45″. *Photo: Daniel Hopper*

Tornado Chandelier

Tornado chandelier is a twisted, undulating steel form. It is meant to be a visual roller-coaster ride around the light and energy of 75 candles. After creating a scale model of the chandelier, I built the full-sized version clamped to a freestanding lift in the shop. The final suspension technique uses three cables attached to a winch system. The balance of the chandelier was never tested until the form was complete. Only an intuitive feeling for the distribution of the steel's weight informed its construction, and, my intuition was correct. The main form was created using 1"-2" tube and 1/4"-1" solid steel. Since this was my first extensive use of tube, I laboriously cut the tube into 3' lengths, filled them with sand, capped each end and forged my tapers. Now, thanks to the help of a fellow blacksmith, I achieve the same effect more quickly using a die on my power hammer.

Daniel Hopper. *Tornado.* Chandelier. 2006. Steel, wax candles. 4' x 5' x 7'. *Photo: Robert Emery Smith*

Fireplace Screen

Two screens were required for this pass-through fireplace. It was important that there was no visual interference between that viewer and the fire itself. This meant replacing a large area of the door, where screen would have been, with glass, leaving a thin strip of screen at the top for ventilation. It also meant placing the design elements at the edge, to frame the fire. The 1" x 1" steel bar framework provided a solid physical counterbalance to the lighter, more airy, visual effect of the ornamentation. The custom offset pivots made for a cleaner design, removing any large hinges that would create visual interruption on the inside wall of the fireplace.

Daniel Hopper. Fireplace Screen. 2008. Steel and glass. 28" x 36-1/2". *Photo: Daniel Hopper*

Fireplace Tools

The challenge in designing these fireplace tools was to match the setting in which they lived. The client's home is minimally furnished, yet every object is as beautiful to look at as it is to use. Tucked up in the hills and almost hovering in the trees, it was easy to adapt my personal aesthetic to theirs, as my style is to derive form from nature. I designed the tools to mimic antlers because the tips of the antlers lent an easy representation of poker ends as well as the tie-in of nature to the client's interior space. I have always loved the feel of bumpy antler ends in the palm of my hand. I wanted that feel to be a major component in the interaction with the tools. Due to the room's layout, it would have been intrusive to have the usual stand for the toolset. Instead, there was an existing stone shelf within the fireplace that accommodated the tools perfectly, so I designed a cradle to keep them nestled together.

Daniel Hopper. Fireplace Tools. 2010. Steel and whiskbroom. 26", 24", 17" & 11" long. *Photo: Daniel Hopper* (opposite page)

Fireplace Tools Cradle

Design considerations for the room required this fireplace tool set to lay on a stone shelf rather than stand upright. I didn't want the tools to have a cluttered, tossed to the side quality, so I designed a cradle to visually tie all three tools together as a set. For the texture on the ends of the "antlers" I used a tree-texture die that I made for a previous project. I then TIG welded small balls of filler rod onto the ridges, heated with a torch, and wire wheeled all of it to soften up any harsh edges and make it comfortable to the touch. When that was completed, I heated up the last 3/4" of the steel and worked the end with a pneumatic hammer to upset and indent the end.

Daniel Hopper. Fireplace Tools Cradle. 2010. Steel. 11" x 7" x 4". *Photo: Daniel Hopper*

Intracoastal Iron LLC

Ben Kastner, Richard Coley, and Shane Urquhart

Wilmington, North Carolina

Individual Artwork

Intracoastal Iron. Railing. Murphy Residence. Mild steel swaged on the diamond with forged brackets. Hunt room: 1 1/4″ x 1 1/4″. *Photo: Ed Kelly*

Intracoastal Iron. Exterior railing. Shaw Residence. Forged. 200′ plus 5/8″ x 5/8″ forged scrollwork. *Photo: Ed Kelly*

Intracoastal Iron. Main Railing. Murphy Residence. 110′ of interior rail, swaged double cap rail with forged octagonal pickets made from 1 1/4″ x 1 1/4″ to match wood columns. The pickets are joined to the cap rail with countersunk rivets. *Photo: Ed Kelly*

Ben Kastner. *Experiment 1.* Traditional mortise and tenon joinery techniques with copper nails. Mild steel forged. 3/4″ x 3/4″. *Photo: Ed Kelly*

Benjamin Hamilton Isaiah

Tempe, Arizona, bbbennn@gmail.com

Artist's Statement

My process is not always deliberate. I embrace serendipity and avoid forced expression. Inspiration comes from life, the natural world, and my existence, spiritual and physical, real and surreal. I fell in love with metal's solidity, diverse auras, and permanent qualities. Metal can be a seductive focal point or the perfect framework for integrating leather, stones, and found or recycled objects.

Individual Artwork

Benjamin H. Isaiah. *Stand Up.* 2005. Forged and welded. Iron and steel. Wrapped iron with a jagged circular top bowl. 4' h. *Photos: artist*

Benjamin H. Isaiah. *Two Heads.* Leather bound hatchet head on brown haft. 2009.
Pattern welded steel leather and Palo Verde wood. 2′ l x 10″ w. *Photos: Tedd McDonah*

Frank Jackson

Clovis, California, frankjacksonforge@yahoo.com

Individual Artwork

Cross

This cross was the culmination of three days of texture and twisting, design and exploration.

Frank Jackson. *Cross.* 5′ x 3′.

Bird and Oak Mirror

I forged and fabricated this mirror for my big brother Mike, who is fourteen years older than me. As a child, growing up in Miami, Florida, Mike would take me to the beach, the zoo, the museum of natural history, and fishing in the Florida Keys.

Frank Jackson. *Bird and Oak Mirror*.

Bookshelf

I wanted an artistic bookshelf to house my blacksmith reference books. The top shelf is marble.

Frank Jackson. Bookshelf.

Jake James

Sooke, British Columbia, jake@jakejames.ca

Artist's Statement

Jake has built his shop and his work ethos around the ideal that the hearth and anvil are the very heart of everything he does. Each project is designed to showcase the elegant and expressive nature of hot forged steel.

Individual Artwork

Steel and Glass Railing

The use of hot riveted structural posts bring classic forged joinery to an ultra-modern format.

Jake James. Steel and Glass Railing. *Photo: Jeffery Bosdet*

Lotus Railing

Section of an extensive railing project showing the interesting solution to the 4″ code rule.

Jake James. *Lotus.* Railing. *Photo: Merle Proflofsky*

The Cyclist

Whimsical public sculpture capturing the modern bohemian feel of the James Bay community in Victoria, BC.

Jake James. *The Cyclist*. Sculpture. *Photo: Federico Vanoli*

Bamboo Gate

Jake James. Bamboo Gate. Forged. Steel. Rust patina. *Photo: Federico Vanoli*

Sue Lampert

Jupiter, Florida, ironshorestudio@gmail.com

Individual Artwork

Birds in Paradise Waterfall Sculpture
Sculpture detail is true to size.

Sue Lampert. *Birds in Paradise*. Sculpture. Forged and fabricated all aluminum waterfall sculpture. Primed and painted finish. 36″ w x 72″ h.

Wetlands

All aluminum waterfall sculpture inspired by the vast and beautiful wetlands here in Florida.

Sue Lampert. *Wetlands.* Hand forging, chasing, repoussé, modern fabrication, and welding. Faux finish. 7′ w x 7′ h.

Door Grilles

Grilles are hinged to open for cleaning glass. The trick was to create a design that would open without interference with the client's lever handles.

Sue Lampert. Door Grilles. Forged and fabricated bronze. Deep bronze patina finish and waxed to match the client's hardware. Each grille weighs 83 lbs. 6′ w x 8′ h. Private residence.

Sue Lampert. Calla Lily Console Table. Forged, chased, and fabricated steel with contoured marble top. Faux finish. 45″ w x 34″ h. Private residence.

Shawn Lovell

Berkeley, California, shawn@slmetalworks.com

Shawn Lovell at work.

Individual Artwork

1st Congregational Church of San Francisco Sanctuary Doors

The leaves, scrolls, fruit, and other elements were hammered out of solid square bar stock and then fused together using an ancient technique know as forge welding. In order to forge weld, the elements are held together in the coal fire until they reach a near white heat (between 2400-2800 degrees Fahrenheit) They are then placed on the anvil and fused together with quick, light hammer blows.

For the flower elements, colored glass is fused into holes punched into the steel. I soften the glass cane (cane is glass rod) with a torch to form a gather (a blob on the end about the size of a large grape) and manipulate (slump) it into the hole I have punched and leave it to cool slowly in an insulated material (such as vermiculite).

Shawn Lovell. 1st Congregational Church of San Francisco Sanctuary Doors. 2008.
Forged and fabricated. Steel, fused glass. 9′ h x 6′ 3″ w. *Photos: Anita Bowen*

Fireplace Surround

The leaves, scrolls, and other elements were forged out of solid square bar stock and then joined together by heating them to fusing temperature in the coal forge and then hammering them together at the anvil.

Shawn Lovell. Fireplace surround in process. 2008.

Shawn Lovell. Fireplace surround. 2008. Forged steel. 37″ h x 34″ w.

Interior Guard Railing

The leaves scrolls and other elements were forged out of solid square bar stock. They are joined by heating them to fusing temperature in the coal forge and then hammering them together at the anvil. The remaining elements were joined using rivets tenons and collars.

Shawn Lovell. Interior Guard Railing. 2008. Forged steel. 15′ l.

Susan Madacsi

Ledyard, Connecticut, smadacsi@earthlink.net

Artist's Statement

Texture, color, and form contribute greatly when I am developing a piece. My color process involves layers of pigment and wax, which have been gently taken down with various abrasives to reveal layers of color and steel. Each "tile" or "block" is individually forged on a power hammer using patterns of movement to create complex textures. These techniques help to underline the clay-like qualities of steel as it is transformed during the forging process.

Individual Artwork

Great Room Double Doors Fire Screen

The clients of this project were looking for a design that complimented the Swedish Chalet architectural style of their home. This is a double door screen built to open and reveal a second interior screen with copper mesh. The door faces are built up in layers using techniques including piercing and hand filing using a coping saw, upsetting and chamfering edges, riveting, chiseling, and filing.

The four-piece tool set includes a shovel made from a solid piece of 5/8" x 2" bar. The shovel scoop was spread thin and wide. I then used a hand sketched pattern to compliment the aesthetics of the screen, transferred the form on the "sheet" at the end of the bar, and I then chisel cut the shape.

Using the same chisel, I scored lines to use as folding references to create the edges of the scoop. There is a pair of tongs, along with a poker and a broom as well. I sent the broom handle to a broom maker to insure there was a confluence of craftsmanship and authenticity of work. (opposite page)

Susan Madacsi. *Hoestra Great Room Fire Screen*. 2007. Forged and fabricated. Steel, wax, mica, borosilicate glass. *Photo: Larry St. Pierre*

Untitled

Susan Madacsi. *Untitled.* Pedestal piece. 2009. Forged and fabricated. Steel, enamel paints, and wax. 38″ l x 24″ w x 16″ h. *Photo: Ralph Phil*

Blue Cloud

Susan Madacsi. *Blue Cloud.* Wall hung sculpture. 2010. Forged and fabricated. Steel, enamel paints, and wax. 44″ l x 34″ h. *Photo: Larry St. Pierre*

Grand Confectioner's Vessel

Susan Madacsi. *Grand Confectioner's Vessel.* Pedestal piece. 2010. Forged and fabricated. Steel, enamel paints, and wax. 24" l x 24" w x 8" h. *Photo: Larry St. Pierre*

Wabi Sabi Vessel

Susan Madacsi. *Wabi Sabi Vessel.* Pedestal piece. 2011. Forged and fabricated. Steel, enamel paints, and wax. 10" diameter. *Photo: Larry St. Pierre*

Marc Maiorana

Cedar Bluff, Virginia, marcmaiorana@hotmail.com

Individual Artwork

Marc Maiorana. *Penland Grand Rail*. 2006. Formed steel. 26′ x 3′ x 1′.

Marc Maiorana. *Andiron*. 2009. Formed steel. 20″ x 20″ x 18″.

Marc Maiorana. *Arthur Gate*. 2010. Formed steel. 60″ x 60″ x 6″.

Manuka Forge

Cochrane, Alberta, Canada, www.manukaforge.ca

Artist's Statement

Hot forging, working the metal, directing the movement, and capturing the moment, liberating the inherent biotic nature of the seemingly inert steel ... this is my art.

Individual Artwork

Manuka Forge: John Monteath & Brenda Field. Balcony Railing and Front Door Grilles, with copper detail, and Stair Hand Rails. 2004-2005. Hand forged and fabricated with a paint finish. Copper-chased and repoussé. Mild steel. Railing: 24′ x 42″; door grilles: 96″ x 30″ each; hand rails: 56″ x 36″.

Manuka Forge: John Monteath & Brenda Field. Interior Residential Stair Railing. 2007-2009. Hand forged and fabricated. Mild steel, black linseed oil finish. 150′ x 36″. (above and next page)

Manuka Forge

Manuka Forge: John Monteath & Brenda Field. Built In Fireplace Doors with Iris Detail. 2007-2009. Hand forged and fabricated. Mild steel, linseed oil finish. 36" x 40".

Moryx Crakewood and GMO.9

These two pieces were conceived of and created in the weeks after reading Margaret Atwood's dystopian, post apocalyptic novel *Oryx and Crake*. These pieces are one and two in a series.

Manuka Forge: John Monteath. *Moryx Crakewood* (left) and *GMO.9* (right). Standing floor sculptures. 2009. Hand forged, fire welded, riveted, and fabricated mild steel, forged and fold formed copper, sandstone. 69" x 24" x 19" and 76" x 23" x 16".

Darrell Markewitz

Ontario, Canada

Individual Artwork

Railings

These railings were designed in keeping with the original Arts & Crafts style home (built in the 1920s): clean lines, obviously forged elements, and sweeping curves. The top handrails are slightly collapsed 1 1/2″ thick walled square tube. The individual support elements are forged from 3/8 thick by 1 1/2 wide flat stock. In final position, the individual curved elements interlace as they cross over each other. The quality of the individual elements is subtle, but immediately visible, in keeping with the subdued good taste of the entire home.

Darrell Markewitz. Railing. Richards House, Toronto. 2009. Forged bar and structural mild steel. Five joined panels, the longest roughly five feet.

Door Grill

This decorative grill panel was intended to add extra security over a narrow glass panel set into the original front door of an early 1960s bungalow. Forged from steel pipe, a spray of curved elements each grips a large glass disk. These elements are securely held by passing through holes hot punched into two flat bars. In the end, the customers liked the piece so much that they purchased this new solid white steel door—to better show off the work!

Darrell Markewitz. Door Grill. Graham House, Guelph. 2009. Forged structural mild steel, commercial glass. Roughly 66" x 24".

Segmented Urn

The body of the urn is composed of a number of individually hand-forged strips of antique wrought iron (recycled from a bridge built in Ohio about 1860). I saw samples of the basic technique used here at a workshop / demonstration by the Japanese blacksmith, Takayoshi Komine. The individual elements are forged to shape, then MIG welded along one edge to create the sealed container.

Actual historic wrought iron has been chosen for the construction because of its excellent forging characteristics and special durability. The metal itself is already some 150 years old, and should easily endure for centuries more. Intended as a funeral urn, it provides a fitting resting place for the memories of one passed beyond us.

Darrell Markewitz. *Segmented Urn.* 2008. Forged and fabricated antique wrought iron, copper plate. About 6" x 6" x 18" h (weight about 40 lbs).

Matthew and Karine Maynard

Lawrenceburg, Kentucky, www.maynardstudios.com

Individual Artwork

Basket Weave Rail

The inspiration for this railing started with a box of components found years ago by the client in the back of a closing business. This commission was a close collaboration with the client spanning over a year and a half from first thoughts to fruition.

Matthew & Karine Maynard. *Basket Weave Rail.* Forged, welded, and formed. Wire-brushed with clear enamel finish. Mild steel & antique stamped components. *Photo: Ryan Bowles*

Tree House Railing

The inspiration for this railing came from the client's memories of playing in the woods as a child. The railing's whimsical design recalls these experiences. The steel is forged and formed to fit the cedar hand grip, which is an assembly of six individual pieces lap jointed, glued, and doweled together. The newel post was forged from 2-inch solid square stock.

Matthew & Karine Maynard. *Tree House Railing.* 2008. Forged, welded, and riveted. Wire-brushed with clear enamel finish. Mild steel with hand worked cedar handgrip. *Photo: artist*

Kitchen Railing

The tread width for this staircase was greater than five feet, requiring handgrips on both sides. To find a creative solution, rather than a single handgrip with simple brackets, the wall-mounted portion of this railing was approached as an individual railing in itself. The newel post was built up in layers and sized to have definite presence in the room, with a large bundle of tapered and twisted round stock forming the upper portion of the post. The ribbon drops were placed to allow a grasping point for the lowest tread.

Matthew & Karine Maynard. *Kitchen Railing.* 2009. Forged & welded mild steel, Brazilian Cherry cap rail with hand-carved terminal. Wire-brushed with clear enamel finish. Polychromatic highlights and Gilder's paste.

Nashville, Main Rail

At over 160 feet in length and residing in a large space, the newel posts of this floating curved staircase were designed to be a solid trunk from which the rest of the metalwork could emerge. Surrounding elements within the home were echoed in details, including copper, brass, stone, and wood.

Matthew & Karine Maynard. *Nashville, Main Rail.* 2009. Forged, welded, and lathe turned pieces, hand-formed leaves, inlaid marble accents and burled maple components with design details done in pyrography. Mild steel, bronze, brass, Brazilian Cherry, Burled Maple, copper, & marble. Wire-brushed with clear enamel finish. *Photos: artist*

Craftsman Railing

This railing was designed to complement the Craftsman style with hints of French Country. All pieces were forged and the horizontal members were punched and drifted to allow the passing through of vertical members. The convex handgrip is forged bronze.

Matthew & Karine Maynard. *Craftsman Railing.* 2010. Forged & welded. Wire-brushed with clear enamel finish. Mild steel & bronze. *Photos: Ryan Bowles*

David McCord

Elora, Ontario, Canada, artistinmetal@yahoo.ca

Artist's Statement

If there is beauty in my work, credit must be shared with the natural properties of the material, and the traditional methods of the blacksmith. The style may be contemporary, but the medium and traditions have equal input.

Traditional forging has a directness that is lacking in a lot of other methods. If you work with it, I think you will find that the great physical strength you hear about is not really necessary. With practice you can produce work that balances the masculine and the feminine. The material is just too stubborn to be ruled by brute force.

Individual Artwork

Copper Bowls

A simple but satisfying project: A disk of copper with a wired edge is sunk into a sandbag, planished on the anvil, and colored with heat. Being color blind, I don't quite get it, but it makes other people happy.

David McCord. Copper Bowls. 13″ - 24″ dia.

Bench

This was commissioned as a memorial for the client's father, and placed on the grounds of the Elora Centre for the Arts. This project was a good example of the pure terror of a blank sheet of paper. I couldn't come up with any ideas that were any good, until the client showed me a photo of something she had seen in Europe. Then this idea came rushing out. The photo was of a casting, but by modifying it to obey the principals of forging, a pleasing bench was produced.

David McCord. Bench.

Door Pull

The technical requirements for this pull, a birthday present for a good friend and gallery owner, were small; it is mostly just free forging. Flat bar was tapered on both ends, and then beveled on one side in the middle. Two mortise and tenon joints were used for the mounting posts. Several layers of oil paint highlighted with aluminum provide the finish.

David McCord. Door pull. 30" x 8".

Gates

This was the first job that I did using my fly press. I did the slitting and the offset for the pass through with the press. I learned about lefts and rights, and the trap of thinking the fitting would be easy because I drove right by the site most days. I did not subtract the thickness of the hinge plates. Taking the time to make proper story poles, or a temporary frame, would have solved that problem.

David McCord. Gates. 48″ x 44″.

Table with Sandstone Top

The legs were forged by upsetting and tapering. Each stretcher is held by a collar and the wrap. The finish is clear urethane.

Table

This is a simple table, with three mortise and tenon legs, and a round banded steel top.

David McCord. Table with Sandstone Top. 18″ x 18″ x 26″.

David McCord. Table. 26″ h x 16″ dia.

Randy McDaniel

Reading, Pennsylvania, rams4g@msn.com

Individual Artwork

Pysanky Egg

Problem solving is a big part of what we do. A client wants a 22" diameter egg, plus a traditional Ukrainian design! Not only is it a sign, but they would like to put a light in the bottom of it. Not only did I have to create the eggs, but also two forms for shaping the metal from the inside and the outside. Here my design skill with AutoCAD, combined with a laser cutting company, enabled what years earlier would have been impossible. They laser cut out the front and back design and the parts needed to construct the forms required to shape the egg. Then it was just a matter of hot forging the egg pattern to shape and finishing the details. Fun!

Randy McDaniel. *Pysanky Egg.* Sculptural lamp/sign. 2006. Hot sinking a laser cut design and hand cutting and forming the sides. Pedestal: built up of rolled steel tubing. Forged laser cut steel plate and tubing. 79" h x 22" dia. *Photo: Randy McDaniel*

Clayed 602

I have been on a journey of about seven years trying to find out how some locally made steel tiles were produced. A smith who died years before made them and all of his equipment was auctioned off. The only things left were some floor lamps and some forged steel tiles. I was fortunate enough to obtain these tiles. Looking on the back of them I can see the telltale signs of hot work. So how did he make each one identical to the others? The smith must have used hand forged dies, but in what piece of equipment? I first tried my power hammer, which bounced the plate around, giving me line echoes. So I tried a huge kick press—not enough power to make the impression. I purchased an old drop hammer. Even dropping a seventy-five pound weight six feet wasn't enough power. Then I saw the knife makers using a hydraulic forging press that they were building themselves. That did it! It squishes a plate into dies and much more. I went to a local smith who makes damascus steel for the knife makers as I had heard that he uses three presses in his shop that he built himself. I figured I could learn what was involved in building a press. He had a double cylinder press in the shed that he started and hadn't finished. I bought that one from him and complete the build with his assistance. Since then I have been creating tooling in the form of texturing dies, punches, and specialized tooling. One of the things that I love the most about this machine is that it pushes hot metal, steel, bronze, and titanium, as if it were a piece of clay in my hands. This piece is a good example. It looks like I put my thumbs into it and pushed down, squishing the material down and outward.

Randy McDaniel. *Clayed 602.* Sculpture. 2009. Hot forged on a 60-ton hydraulic forging press using texture dies and punches. Hot forged pure iron. 2 3/4" h x 4 3/4" square. *Photo: Randy McDaniel*

Cowboy Hat

This is my most recent cowboy hat, with a bit more detail than usual. I've been forging cowboy hats for over twenty years. They are usually forged from a sheet of steel, but I've also made them from damascus steel, copper, and bronze sheet. This hat band started with a piece of wire that was twisted and then flattened. The feather was a piece of 1/4" round stock that was flattened, shaped, and then the details chiseled into it.

Randy McDaniel. *Cowboy Hat.* Sculpture. 2010. Hot sunk and shaped. Forged steel. 1 3/4" h. x 4 5/8" l. x 3 1/4" d. *Photo: Randy McDaniel*

The Hawk

My most recent work of forged art. This was originally designed seven years ago as an exterior piece, mounted on an eight-foot pedestal and with a four-foot wingspan. Creating it as a smaller design was a great way to figure out the intricacies of creating such a piece and in doing so I also found it to be a more personal size.

Randy McDaniel. *The Hawk.* Sculpture. 2010. A progression of laser cut material, solid bar stock, and hydraulically pressed steel. Forged steel. 9 3/4" h x 7 1/2" w x 5 1/2" d. *Photo: Randy McDaniel*

Patrick McIvor

Castlegar, British Columbia, Canada, patmcivor@yahoo.ca

Individual Artwork

Patrick McIvor. *Little Dragon Boat.* Sculpture. 2008. Copper and iron. 12″ x 16″ x 21″. *Photo: J. Anderson of Slocan, Valley, BC*

Patrick McIvor. *The Tear*. Sculpture. 2009. Bronze and steel. 8" x 19" x 21". *Photo: J. Anderson of Slocan, Valley, BC*

Patrick McIvor. *Taking Flight.* Sculpture. 2009. Iron and copper. 30" x 48" x 66". *Photo: Patrick McIvor*

Patrick McIvor. *Skeletal Spawning Salmon*. Sculpture. 2009. Iron, copper, and stone. 27″ x 42″ x 84″. *Photo: Patrick McIvor*

Patrick McIvor

Patrick McIvor. *Warm Welcome Home.* Sculpture. 2010. Iron and river stone. 48″ x 60″ x 73″. *Photo: Courtesy of Dave Gluns, Nelson, BC and Castlegar Sculpture walk, Castlegar, BC*

Patrick McIvor. *Buffalo Hunt.* Sculpture. 2009. Bronze and wood. 36″ x 48″. *Photo: Patrick McIvor*

Michael Migala

Harvard, Illinois, migalametals@msn.com

Artist's Statement

My aesthetic inspiration comes from recognizing subtle visual elements in natural and industrial environments and capturing the essence of these details in my work. Through the use of form, structure, texture, connection devices, and patination, I render images in metal that are a response to my observations. I am drawn to the process of taking a dense, unyielding material and forcefully transforming it into a graceful object, which can be functional as well, as sculptural. These are the challenges that invigorate my creative pursuits.

Individual Artwork

Grand Staircase

This is a custom designed, entirely hand forged grand staircase. The top center section was built and installed first to establish a base point from which to build the stair rail. The stair rail framework was built on site over the course of four days. Several days of preparation were needed at the shop to create the posts and pre-curve the top and bottom frame material. The framework was welded into four sections (each side) that were mechanically fastened together. It was disassembled and taken back to the shop. We then forged all of the decorative elements, welded them together, and did all of the finish work. Finish is sandblasted, chemically gun blued, and hand rubbed to bring out the forged texture. A clear coat lacquer is then applied. Installation of the entire staircase took less than a day.

Michael Migala. Grand Staircase. Hand forged, welded, sandblasted finish, chemically gun blued, hand rubbed, lacquer. (above and opposite page)

Living Room Fire Screen

The frame and decorative elements are steel. Brass rivets and bronze screen. The flowers match examples we created for the grand staircase and railings. They are hand painted. Vases are 1/8″ forged steel. We used paper templates to arrive at their shape. The flowers and vases are attached to the frame with tiny threaded rods. Finish is sandblasted and chemically rusted with a clear lacquer overspray.

Michael Migala. Living Room Fire Screen. Steel, brass rivets, bronze screen.

Jeff Mosher

Johnsonville, New York, mosherunlimited@aol.com

Individual Artwork

Mink Fireplace Scene

It started out that I was asked to build the screen doors; after the doors were done, the customer wanted two mink (standing) as andirons. The idea was to make this fireplace attractive all year long. I had two mink stuffed in the positions I wanted to use as models. I used one piece of 3 x 3 solid square stock about 14″ long for the standing mink and 3″ solid round stock about 14″ long for the mink on all fours. Grinders and hand tools were used to make each mink. Broken fiddle strings became whiskers, melted glass became eyes, and an old rasp created the "raked" body hair.

The fireplace was fairly large, measuring 5′ wide and high, with a depth of 38″. All of the steel is mild steel wrapped around rocks found around the property. The tree trunks are made from well casing with the bark welded on. The branches, vines, and foliage are all hand wrought, as are the dragonflies and frogs.

The fireplace is used on a regular basis, so all the iron had to be of a pretty heavy gauge so as not to warp or burn. The entire piece weighs about 400-500 pounds and is put together like a puzzle in seven pieces.

The gate was formed around the frame and held in place using old milk bottle wire (two pieces twisted together in fifteen foot lengths, then hand sewn in place). The entire project took roughly 600 hours to complete.

Jeff Mosher. Mink Fireplace Scene. Hand wrought and carved. Mild steel. Gate. Traditional joinery. Mild steel.

Tree Lamp

Jeff Mosher. Tree Lamp. Hand forged. Mild steel. Rawhide lampshade. 20″ h x 16″ w.

Balcony

All of the vines, leaves, and flowers are hand forged. The flowers are all copper and brass.

Jeff Mosher. Balcony. Hand forged, traditional joinery. Mild steel, copper, and brass. 18′ l x 5′ d.

Suraiya Murray

Seguin, Texas

Individual Artwork

Photo: Germaine Tuff

Suraiya Murray. Garden Sculpture. 2010. Hand-forged steel sculpture; joinery: mortise & tenon, riveting, and wrapping. 39″ w x 33″ h. *Courtesy Sandra and Wellborn Gregg; Photos: Germaine Tuff; Artist; and Wyatt McSpadden* (left and opposite page)

Photo: Wyatt McSpadden

Photo: Wyatt McSpadden

Matt M. Myers

Macomb, Illinois, matt@mattmyerssculpture.com

Artist's Statement

Thematically my work is about my relationship with nature and the animals and plants that dwell in the woods around my home and studio in rural Illinois. It's not an attempt to copy nature but rather to emulate and investigate it through shape and form.

Individual Artwork

Bird and Snake Sconce

In response to a particularly dark and gloomy winter I started a series of lights to literally and figuratively bring some light into the home. They are all made from recycled metal. The electrical fixtures are the only new materials.

Matt M. Myers. *Bird and Snake Sconce.* Hand forged mild steel with canvas. 24″ x 12″ x 7″. *Photo: Larry Dean*

Garden Fountain

Matt M. Myers. *Garden Fountain*. Hand forged. Mild steel, stainless steel, & carved stone. 42" x 15" x 15". *Photo: Larry Dean*

Gardener's Dream

In this piece I was really just exploring the material, seeing how high I could get the branches and leaves to go before the piece became top heavy. I was also trying new (to me) methods of shaping the hot steel, including chasing and repoussé, as well as building a hollow form with red hot metal.

Matt M. Myers. *Gardener's Dream.* Hand forged. Mild steel. 108" x 14" x 14". *Photo: Larry Dean*

Suspended Pod

With this piece I am responding to the materials. I loved the deeply pitted texture of a section of very old steel pipe I had found. From there I "simply" cut, forged, welded, and ground the pieces until it felt finished. The result is a sort of reliquary, which has yet to find its bones.

The Font

The only part that is not recycled steel is the gold leaf of the inner bowl.

Matt M. Myers. *Suspended Pod.* Hand forged and fabricated. Mild steel. 69" x 36" x 14". *Photo: Larry Dean*

Matt M. Myers. *The Font.* Hand forged. Mild steel and gold leaf. 33" x 21" x 21". *Photo: Larry Dean*

Two Crows

The crows themselves are pieced together from many bits and pieces of scrap.

Matt M. Myers. *Two Crows.* Hand forged. Mild steel. 26″ x 12″ x 14″. *Photo: Larry Dean*

W.R. Nager

Lakeland, Florida, metal8481@verizon.net

Individual Artwork

Flight

Flight was designed as an outdoor sculpture for Tampa International Airport. The two hammered curves were formed and seamed on the top edge with a 3/8″ thick piece of polished acrylic bent and shaped hot by hand and then sandwiched in between. This sculpture is mirror polished, lit from within with red light, and lit from the exterior in red and green. Flight circumscribes the flight path of a plane entering or leaving the airport.

W.R. Nager. *Flight.* 2006. Hammered. Forged stainless steel. Intended size: 19′ h x 47′ l.

Twilight

Twilight is made from hammered stainless steel worked into a double curve, mirror polished, and then married to an adjoining piece of clear acrylic with identical curved lines. Both stainless steel and acrylic contain and reflect light. This is a daytime/nighttime sculpture.

W.R. Nager. *Twilight.* 2006. Hammered. Stainless steel, clear acrylic.

Zachary Noble

Bakersville, North Carolina, info@zacknoble.com

Artist's Statement

The ancient forging process of manipulating the cross section of metal between hammer and anvil allows the blacksmith to shape the metal into limitless designs. When the iron is heated to two thousand degrees it becomes soft like putty and can be stretched or pinched using a variety of tools. The beauty of forged iron is linked directly to the hand of the smith; every hammer blow is moving the metal and leaving its mark. The blacksmith has a responsibility to produce quality work for the sole reason that the iron will record that work long after the smith is dead. Blacksmiths are linked to all the smiths before them through the tools they use and the knowledge that has been passed down. It is for these reasons that quality forged iron, whether contemporary or historic, pays homage to both past and future.

Individual Artwork

Zachary Noble. Florida Railing. 2007. 100′ x 54″ x 8″.
Photo: Boynton Beach Photography

Zachary Noble. Baltimore Gate. 2003. 144″ x 96″ x 5″.
Photo: Robert Creamer

Zachary Noble. Oval Table. 2007. 42″ x 21″ x 20″. *Photo: Mary Vogel*

Zachary Noble. Caged Sconces. 2008. 14″ x 5.5″ x 9″. *Photo: Mary Vogel*

Zachary Noble. Candle Pillar. 2009. 5″ x 18″ x 5″. *Photo: Mary Vogel*

Zachary Noble

Zachary Noble. *Ruth's Rail*. 2010. 12′ x 34″ x 5.5″. *Photo: Mary Vogel*

Chad A. Otis

Northfield, Minnesota, goodhue@cpinternet.com

Individual Artwork

Ironwork Sundial

The steel sundial is approximately 4000 pounds, stands 10 feet tall, and is 11 feet long. I designed it to have a steel brick appearance. Each brick was hand cut and then holes were punched into the steel, next each brick was plug welded onto the sundial. This process was time consuming, but the end result—with no welds showing for the bricks—was worth the effort. I also made ironwork flower baskets for the ends, a handrail, a bench, and the stainless steel numerals that the shadow of the sundial casts upon for time. The sundial is installed at Red Wing High School in Red Wing, Minnesota. I made it for inclusion in the Horvat Ring of Honor Project at the school in 2010.

Chad A. Otis. *Ironwork Sundial*. 2010. 10′ h x 11′ l.

George Parker

Helotes, Texas, george@georgeparkerdesigns.com

Artist's Statement

Steel, with its reputation for strength and permanence, commands a certain respect alone. Combining traditional forging processes with more contemporary metal working techniques, steel is transformed from its original state of cold, linear, rigid lines into fluid, graceful, often organic shapes. The end result is truly a collaboration between artist and medium.

Individual Artwork

George Parker. Memorial, Ranch Cemetery. Forged steel. Natural patina. 38" h x 30" w. *Photos: Artist*

George Parker. Entrance to the Twentieth Century Exhibit Wing. Museum of South Texas History. Forged steel and copper. 118″ w x 44″ h. *Photo: Artist*

George Parker. Ranch Office Chandelier. Forged steel and copper. 60″ w x 72″ h. *Photo: Artist*

Dawn Raines

Austin, Texas, draines@austincc.edu

Artist's Statement

My artwork is more or less figurative. My foundation is mainly in ornamental and architectural ironwork and I consider myself to be part traditional and part modern in my execution and approach as a blacksmith. I enjoy the texture and details that can be created in a piece as well as the presence of process. I like to incorporate traditional techniques and joinery in my work; however, I like the look of clean, fluid lines you find using modern welding and finishing processes. You will find that a lot of my work is organic in content and style.

Individual Artwork

Small Electric Guitar

I included this guitar because it gives readers an idea of where I started. It is part of my history as a blacksmith.

Dawn Raines. *Small Electric Guitar.* Sculpture. 2009. Hand forged. Steel with antique brown finish. Approximately 1′ x 4′ x 1″.

Electric Guitar

Dawn Raines. *Electric Guitar.* Sculpture. 2009. Hand forged. Steel with brass brush highlights. Approximately 1′ x 3′ x 1 1/2″.

Untitled

When I was making this flower vase, I was aiming for a very fluid look. The vase was executed using oxy-fuel welding and heating techniques. The scrolls and vase details were hand forged and finished with an antique brown finish called m38 brown.

Dawn Raines. *Untitled.* Sculpture. 2010. Hand forged. Steel with brass brush highlights and antique brown finish. Approximately 1′ x 1′ x 2 1/2′.

Chris Rand

Minneapolis, Minnesota, chris@coppertopforge.com

Artist's Statement

My work expresses the spirit of invention and imagination. I thrive on solving problems using the creative and logical facilities as if both sides of the brain were one. To this end, I design and build site-specific metalwork that is functional and ornamental. Every object is custom tailored to fit a location and a function; which allows me to create unique solutions and explore my visual language. I aim at creating dynamic compositions and enjoy working within a set of constraints—whether location, client, cost, style or scale.

Individual Artwork

Penthouse Light Fixture

The design intent of this light fixture was to look "alive" from every angle and to be a celebration of three-dimensional metal. Inspired by its location along the river, I wanted the fixture to be like a beacon in the sky or a nautical compass providing direction. After making many copper samples with compound shapes and rolled edges to create volume, I did various lighting scenarios and honed in on the form to create a dance of light shining through to the edges. Thirteen separate pieces of metal were hand formed using repoussé techniques and riveted together as one.

Chris Rand. *Penthouse Light Fixture*. 2009. Copper, glass. 11" x 44" dia. Background railing: John Yust, designer; Robert Walsh, Metalsmith.

Owl Fire

The initial design parameters were to make a fireplace surround that had clean lines, textured metal, and some relation to the client's owl andirons. I wanted to frame the hearth with a fitting design that looked like formalwear or a tuxedo. To keep it minimal, the doors swing from only two hinges and the door handles and lock are seamlessly integrated into the frame. It was made using forged and fabricated processes.

Chris Rand. *Owl Fire*. 2009. Steel. 48" x 35" x 3".

Chandeliers

Using classical and modern elements, the living room design was inspired by the topography of the city below and time-lapse photos of blurred traffic light. I wanted to combine steel in a classic form with gold leafed acrylic to create a strong contrast between dark and light values as well as opacity and transparency. Each fixture was scaled and proportioned to the large rooms and tall ceilings. The dining room chandelier features hand-blown shades, forged chain links, and faceted glass inserts.

Chris Rand. Living Room Chandelier. 2010. Steel, glass, acrylic, gold leaf, brass rivets. 49″ x 49″ x 38″.

Chris Rand. Dining Room Chandelier. 2010. Steel, glass, acrylic, gold leaf, brass rivets. 56″ x 25″ x 48″.

David G. Robertson

Cargill, Ontario, Canada, www.artistblacksmith.com

Artist's Statement

Working with hot metal provides limitless opportunity for long-term self expression. Steel can be formed and shaped into realistic representations that can far outlive the artisan.

Nature provides a continuous source of inspiration for me, with its texture, movement, and graceful long, self-supporting lines. Many of these elements become incorporated into my artwork.

The craft of blacksmithing has grown and become accessible to many people across the globe. This renewed interest has fueled development of both techniques and designs in metal work.

Individual Artwork

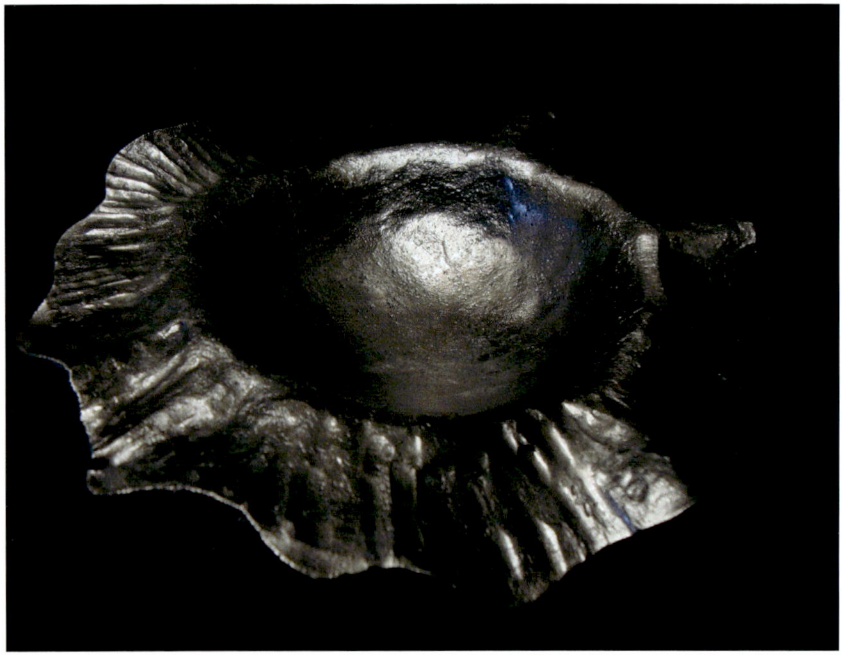

David G. Robertson. Bowl. Forged mild steel plate. Study in stretching and forming. 4″ x 4″ x 1/2″ plate. 8″ diameter. *Photo: artist*

David G. Robertson. *Cross.* Wall mounted cross/wall sculpture. Forged. Mild steel. The heavy texture of the central disk contrasts with the smooth line of the points. 62″ h, 46″ w. *Photos: artist*

Funeral Urn

This urn form was inspired by Chinese gongs. The top disk is hollow with a removable lid to allow the placement of ashes.

David G. Robertson. Funeral Urn. Forged. Mild steel. 27″ h x 24″ w.
Photo: artist

Japanese Flowering Tree in Spring Time

This tree sculpture is heavily textured on the trunk with flowers bursting open.

David G. Robertson. *Japanese Flowering Tree in Spring Time*. Sculpture. Forged and fabricated. Mild steel. 42″ h x 50″ w x 22″ d.
Photos: artist

John Colle Rogers

Oakland, California, johnkojohnkojohnko@yahoo.com

Artist's Statement

I began working steel when I was about nineteen. I was doing my undergrad work in Japanese Studies, and had been making abstract Japanese brush paintings to balance out the academics with some creative play. After a semester in Japan, I returned infused with the direct expressionistic nature of Japanese culture, and I wanted to translate that essence into three dimensions. The aggressive curvilinear forms that resulted got me hooked on forging. To be able to freeze the flow of the steel, and the late night shop ballet—moving from forge to trip hammer to anvil and back—fills me with a calm power that pushes me through work binges even now.

Individual Artwork

Basilisks

The *Basilisk* pieces stem from an interest in gothic armor. The brass and copper elements are ornamental gilding that adds to their savagery or seduction. It is unclear whether the two-headed Basilisks are making love or fighting—they are just pure action. I made these during a pretty tough time in my life, and making the steel do these dark things was a way of externalizing the pain I was feeling, a purification...

John Colle Rogers. *Basilisk 5*. 2005. Forged/cold formed, riveted. Steel, brass, and copper. 21" h. *Photo: artist*

John Colle Rogers. *Basilisk 3*. 2005. Forged/cold formed, riveted. Steel/brass and copper. 18" h. *Photo: artist*

Trouble

Trouble is dynamic in a similar way, but its intent is more purely aggressive. Made from a combination of a shotgun body, AK-47 barrel, all-thread legs, and brass embellishments, it sits poised and distinctly malevolent, despite being the size of a small dog. This piece encapsulates much of my thinking about the compression of will behind much of human endeavor, and how that will can so easily get out of hand.

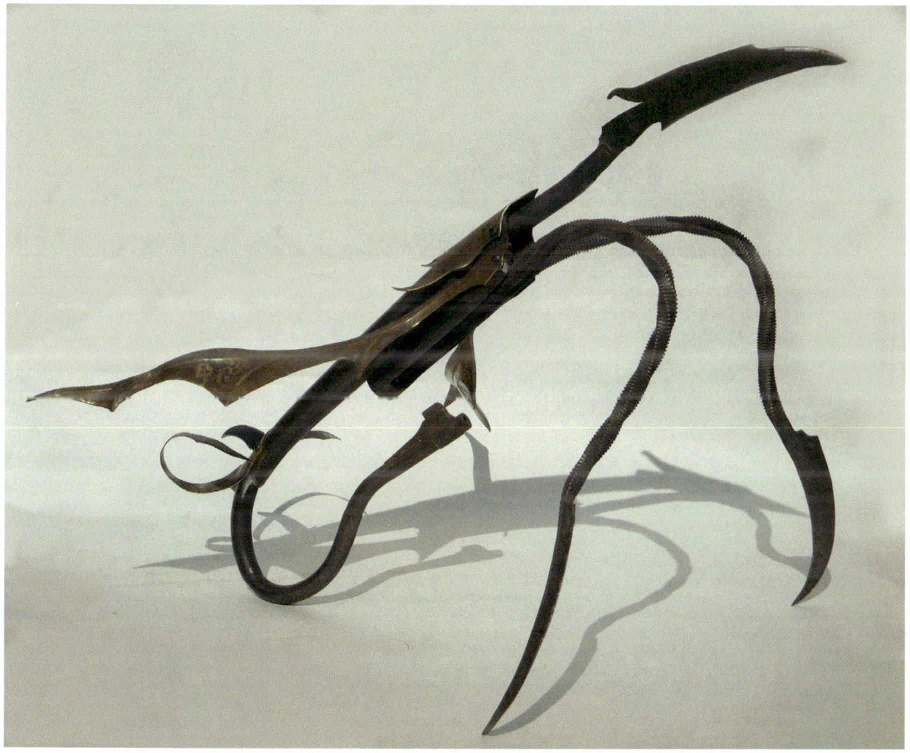

John Colle Rogers. *Trouble*. 2010. Forged/cold formed. Steel bar, all-thread, shotgun receiver, AK-47 barrel, sheet copper. 19" h. *Photo: artist*

Wahoos

The *Wahoos* are a trio of 19'3" wide creatures with the wings of pterodactyls and bodies styled after the Paveway bunker buster bomb. Again, this is a reflection on the possibilities of the hand, compounded by the body's circular center and the bottom facet of the neck being the same dimensions as a banjo. The bird wing evolving into the hand, the possibility for fight or flight or a little tune—these are the mysteries of the Wahoo. These three were installed with five patinaed steel panels on each side, and the green maze-like structure as their target. An abstracted copy of the freeway intersection in the center of Oakland, California, the Maze provides the Wahoos with a sense of focus, and an end to their journey.

John Colle Rogers. *Wahoos*. Installation overview. 2007. Forged and fabricated sheet steel and bar stock. *Wahoos* remain uncoated, panels patinaed with heat and then gun blue. Maze is powder coated. I used heat to "puff" the wings, then an English wheel to solidify the curves. Fingers are 1/2" and 9/16" bar stock with 5/8" and 3/4" ball bearings for knuckles. *Wahoos* have 19'3" wingspans; panels are 5' tall, varying widths. Maze is 6' x 6'. Installation at 21 Grand Gallery, Oakland, California. *Photo: artist*

Street Sign

I have done over forty-five of these pieces for the City and County of San Francisco, in cooperation with the historical Phoenix Iron Works of Oakland, California ("quality castings since 1901"). With PIW providing the cast ball top and the rolled steel pole, and the city contributing the wood sign, my work is to produce the bracket and sign sides. Using a breadth of metalworking techniques from water-jet cutting to forging, I am always proud to make something that will add to the heritage of the City.

John Colle Rogers. *Sign for San Francisco Recreation and Park Dept*. Created with historic Phoenix Iron Works, Oakland, California. 2003-2010. Cast iron ball top, rolled steel pole, forged and fabricated bracket, water-jet cut and fabricated sign sides (wood sign by City). *Photo: artist* (right and opposite page)

HAYES GREEN
SAN FRANCISCO RECREATION
AND PARK DEPARTMENT
488
HAYES

Eric A. Ryser

Manhattan, Kansas, redbeans21@hotmail.com

Artist's Statement: "The Home Front"

While the hours creep across the face, she paces across the hardwood floor. Now she can't even get to sleep since her husband, Tony, left for war. She feels distraught and abandoned by a world she thought she once knew. Emotions are cold beyond comprehension as their little girl turns two. She's left standing on the home front, just the two of them all alone.

Individual Artwork

Eric A. Ryser. *The Home Front*. 2009. Forged, fabricated, and inflated. Mild steel, brass shell casings, wax, and Prismacolor finish. 16" x 14" x 6".

Eric A. Ryser. *Scuba Steve's Combat-Ready Campfire Grill.* 2008. Forged and fabricated steel, found objects, paint and hot wax finish. 45" x 20" x 40".

Eric A. Ryser. *Self Destructive Zones*. 2009. Forged, fabricated, and inflated. Mild steel, brass shell casings, wax, and Prismacolor finish. 21″ x 3.5″.

Eric A. Ryser. *The Righteous Path 1/3.* 2009. Forged. Mild steel, acid etched pattern, Prismacolor. 15″ x .750″.

Eric A. Ryser. *Plate of Peace*. 2010. Forged. Mild steel, acid etched pattern, Prismacolor, barbed wire. 13″ x 13″ x .750″.

Chris Shea

Brandywine, Maryland, chrisshea1@comcast.net

Artist's Statement

I am always intrigued by the echoes of form to be found between the anatomies of human beings, animals, insects, and even plants. The segmented structure of an arthropod, the veined ridges of a fallen leaf, the architecture of a human skeleton—as one reminds me of another, they all remind me how we have evolved together from the same primal materials. I find the thought enormously comforting. In the objects I create, traditional functional forms of furniture and architectural metalwork evolve into new anatomies, drawn from the world around me—both natural and man-made—and expressed in the language of the blacksmith.

Process

Function is where the design process starts. Sketches proceed to measured drawings, to full-scale layouts in the studio. Steel bars and pipes from the steel mill or from my scrap pile (steel is the most recycled material on earth) are heated to glowing, hammered to shape, bent, welded, punched, drilled, etc. Though the process of forging is at the core of my work, it is only the beginning. Grinding, sanding, and hand filing refine the forms. My designs balance freedom and precision. Too little precision and the form won't satisfy my vision for it, or the function will suffer; too much and the energy and movement imparted by the fire's extreme heat and the hammer's violence are refined away.

Separate elements are joined by a variety of means, both traditional and modern. Such elemental kinds of joinery as riveting, forge welding, and mortise-and-tenon joints are among the special joys of the blacksmith's work. Modern electrical welding equipment is also much appreciated. Finally, completed objects are treated with the same care as a woodworker might lavish on an exotic hardwood. To protect the patina and add luster, all metal surfaces are hand-rubbed with many coats of natural oil finish and paste wax.

Special cast or slumped glass elements are created in collaboration with the skilled and talented artist of the Washington Glass Studio.

Individual Artwork

Wasp-waist Console Table

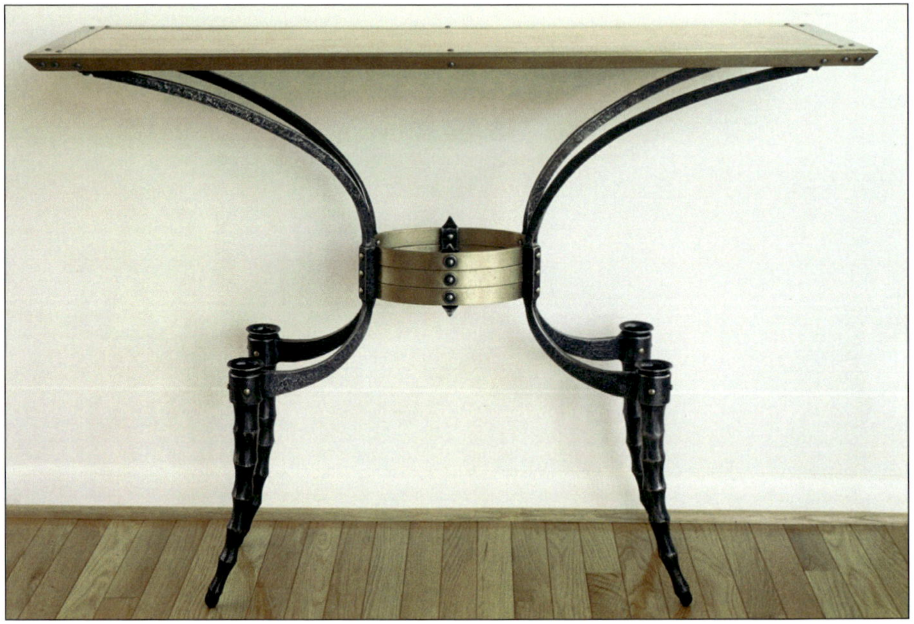

Chris Shea. *Wasp-waist Console Table.* 2001. Forged steel, bronze, cherry. 32″ x 44″ x 14″.

Arthropod Side Table

The legs are forged from steel pipe under a mechanical power hammer. The glass is cast using the dry plaster method to create a texture that complements the weathered surface of the forged metal.

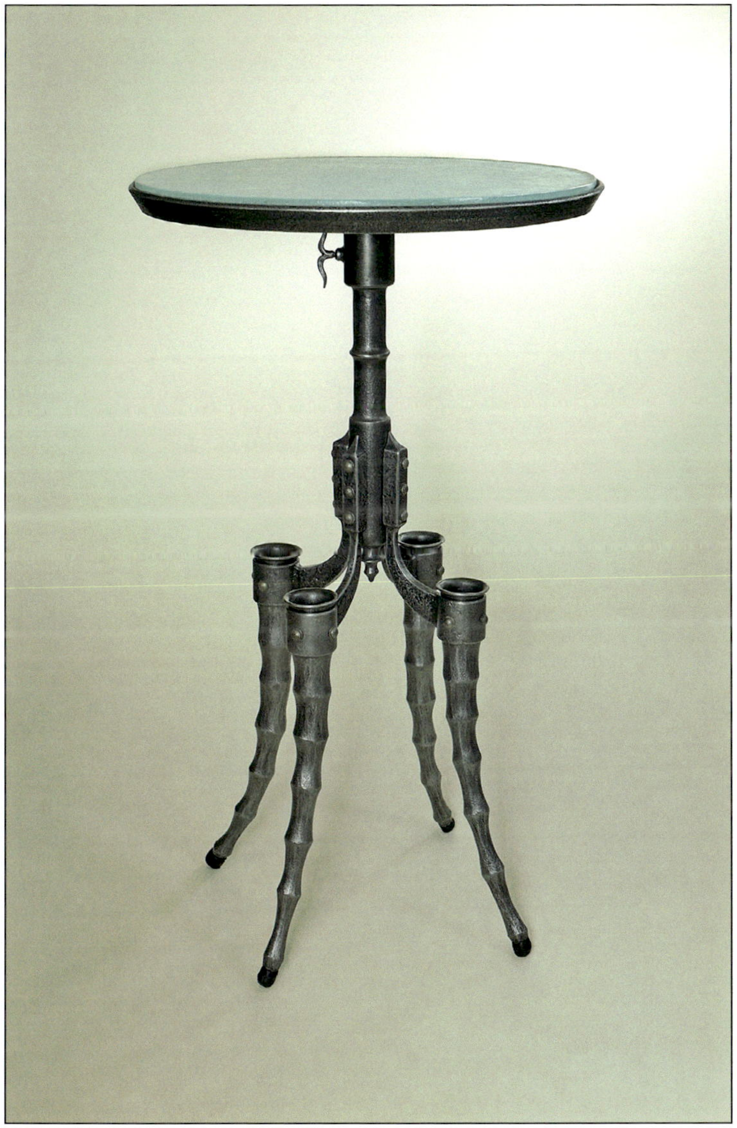

Chris Shea. *Arthropod Side Table*. 2007. Forged steel, cast glass. 30″ x 18″ x 18″.

Café Chair

Chris Shea. *Cafe Chair.* 2007. Forged steel, cast glass. 36″ x 17″ x 17″. *Photo: Griffin Graphics*

Jewelry Display Sconce

There is provision for storing/displaying earrings, necklaces, bracelets or rings.

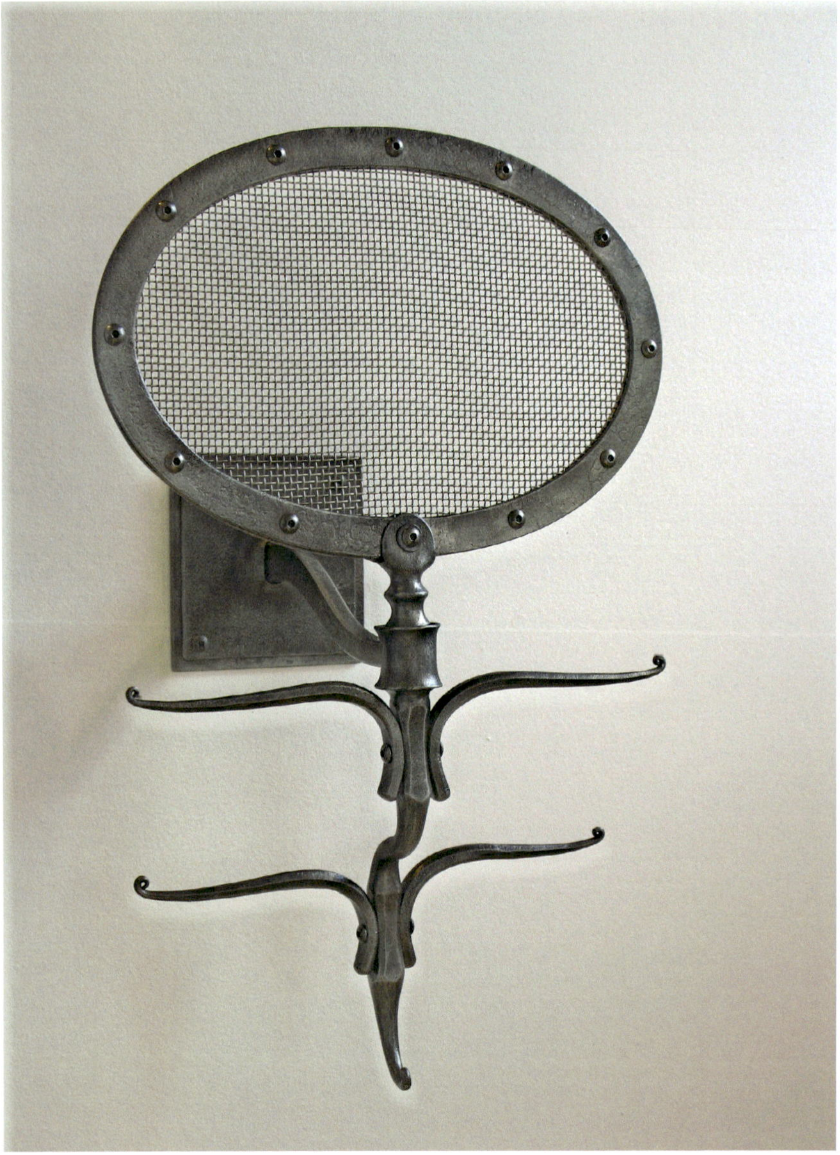

Chris Shea. *Jewelry Display Sconce*. 2008. Forged steel, stainless steel screen. 15" h x 12" x 7".

Symbiotic Variation #1

The design is inspired by forms I find growing together in the woods around my studio: vines, odd mushrooms, and nests.

Chris Shea. *Symbiotic Variation #1.* 2010. Forged steel. 11" x 15" x 4" (w/o candles). *Photo: Anything Photographic*

Erikson Railings

This pair of railings was commissioned by a client whose instructions were merely that she wanted two railings and that symmetry among the two was not required. The designs, inspired by the profusion of plants around the front steps, echo each other in their overall lines but differ markedly in the details. On the right, the implied motion of the intertwined forms flows downward from the front door. On the left, the motion is ascending.

Chris Shea. *Erickson Railings.* 2008.
Forged steel, paint. 36″ x 96″ x 6″.

Jon Shearin

Bakersville, North Carolina, jshearin2004@yahoo.com

Artist's Statement

I strive to make objects that reflect the impact and deterioration of time. From creatures that never existed to the remnants of an imagined world, I strive to manipulate the metal to form objects I want to see come into being. Gaining the ability to sculpt such a rigid and cold material into a piece with its own elastic language has become both a challenge and an ambition. I find that the pairing of the soft forms with traditionally crafted ironwork is a very intriguing combination. I try to balance these two styles so that the resulting piece becomes stronger as a whole.

Individual Artwork

Untitled

I first took a section of perforated sheet steel I found at a local scrap yard and hot rolled it into a cylinder, welded it together, ground down the weld seam, and forged it as I would a regular piece of steel pipe. The necking was done under the power hammer while the tapered bottom and flared top was all done by hand. I then welded the bottom together. The dark gray color on the outside of the vessel is from the forge heat, while the white is enamel paint.

Jon Shearin. *Untitled.* 2009. Forged and fabricated. Mild steel. 12″ x 8″ x 24″. *Photo: artist*

Diamond Aryballos

I used a section of large steel pipe to create both the bowl and lid for this cauldron. The interior of both pieces was filled with chrome plated brass fixtures that, when closed and viewed from above, gives the illusion of a never-ending mosaic of reflected light.

Jon Shearin. *Diamond Aryballos.* 2008. Forged and fabricated. Mild steel, chrome-plated brass. 7″ x 7″ x 8″. *Photos: Tom Mills*

Mica Broch

This piece is also made from steel pipe. I tapered the two ends by hand, welded them shut, and necked down the middle under the power hammer. I cut 2 windows on opposite sides of the top and bottom, formed 1/2" angle iron into frames, and took chips of mica and layered them to create a sheet that was then inserted into the piece. The title comes from the name of a type of ancient Scottish tower used to watch for incoming attacks.

Jon Shearin. *Mica Broch.* 2008. Forged and fabricated. Mild steel, mica. 5" x 5" x 22". *Photos: Tom Mills*

Penland Railing

I was commissioned by the Penland School of Crafts in Penland, North Carolina, to create a railing for a stone path on the main campus. Since I was installing decades after the installation of the walkway and stairs, I wanted to make something that looks as if it had been naturally growing there for years. Installing well after the fact also meant that I had the unique opportunity of not having to deal with the restrictions of building codes. This allowed me to design a railing that didn't need to have a grill-like structure underneath the handrail. I was then able to develop ideas of a freestanding sculpture that can be used as a support for walking instead of designing a frieze that would support a traditional railing. We decided on the idea of fluid, organic branches strapped together that seem to sprout from the ground. The three sections lining the walkway have the sense of plants connected to the surrounding forest, where as the piece for the main stair is one that has broken away and is crawling its way down the stones. I was able to create all the pieces almost entirely out of steel pipe, including the collaring and the installation supports. I used the power hammer to flatten the handrails and collars, to taper the legs, and to sculpt the feet. The pieces were then fabricated together, wire brushed, and repeatedly waxed and buffed for a satin finish. The wax finish has allowed the pieces to breathe and age, further blending them into their surroundings.

Jon Shearin. *Penland Railing*. Forged and fabricated. Mild steel. Four pieces ranging from 7'-12' x 34" x 9". *Photo: Artist*

John Boyd Smith

Roebuck, South Carolina, flemingsmith@aol.com

Artist's Statement

As a young child, I watched my mother nurture plants, flowers, and animals. Her keen interest in nature and the outdoors have had a profound influence on me; I now forge, shape, and sculpt solid steel into forms that emulate the natural world. I have fashioned various flowers, plants, animals, trees, and insects from hot-forged steel for over thirty years. I characterize my style of artistry as "realism in metal" and attempt to depict realism by capturing key details from nature.

Individual Artwork

Swimming Pool Rail

My original metalwork designs often exhibit Low Country themes with marsh birds, sea oats, palmettos, and cattails intertwined in a fluid design to harmonize with nature. From the Florida Keys to Georgia's Barrier Islands and the Carolinas, my work pays homage to these pristine coastal regions.

John Boyd Smith. Swimming pool rail. Hand-forged. Steel.

Chandelier, Pool Table Lighting, and Balcony

This great room features a large chandelier and pool table lighting. The chandelier and balcony ensemble reflects the Low Country style with egrets, fish, frogs, cattails, lily pads, palmettos, and marsh grasses forged in steel to create a hunting lodge inspired residence. My wife, the artist Rhonda Nell Fleming, draws our original concepts and I execute them according to the design plan using a free-form creative style. The wrought iron creations were faux-painted to achieve a bronze patina.

John Boyd Smith. Chandelier, Pool Table Lighting, and Balcony.

Newel, Ascending Staircase, and Second Floor Railing

I was a sculptor prior to becoming a blacksmith and learned that proper scale is the key to a successful concept. Huge Italian marble columns set the tone for this staircase and balcony railing designs. If a delicate openwork design had been created here, it would have been lost in the foyer's massive architecture. Thick, flowing branches combine with twisted pickets to create a formal, organic feeling. Iron was left in its natural state—a color likened to silver or pewter—and is ideal for indoor projects. The finish was created by polishing the raw metal with a coat of linseed oil and wax to preserve its beautiful sheen.

John Boyd Smith. Newel, Ascending Staircase, and Second Floor Railing.

Sconce

This forged steel sconce features bundled palmetto fronds in a faux-bronze patina. They were built for a coastal residence in South Carolina to complement the main staircase railing forged with the same Low Country motifs.

John Boyd Smith. Sconce. Forged steel.

John Boyd Smith. Newel, Ascending Staircase, and Second Floor Railing.

Mike Sohikian

Genoa, Ohio, Sohikian@aol.com

Artist's Statement

Forging and fabricating steel offers me unlimited possibilities to communicate my thoughts and visions to others.

Individual Artwork

The Four Winds

This sculpture is a kinetic wind vane. The Japanese characters on the base represent "the four winds." The mythical nymph surrenders herself to whatever direction the wind takes her.

Mike Sohikian. *The Four Winds.* Kinetic Wind Vane. 2010. Cold forged and fabricated. Steel: recycled a36 and 304 stainless steel, acid stained concrete. 12′ x 9′.

Triomphé

Triomphé represents the conflicting emotions of jubilation and "fear of expectation" that comes with success. The arms are composed of surface bonding cement on a steel armature.

Mike Sohikian. *Triomphé*. Figurative Sculpture. 2010. Fabricated. Recycled a36 steel, concrete, stone. 12′ 6″ h x 4′ 6″ dia. 1000 lbs.

Confessions

This sculpture is subject to the viewer's interpretation.

Mike Sohikian. *Confessions.* Abstract Figures (3 elements). 2008. Fabricated from recycled sch.# 40 pipe, k1107 h.s. concrete castings acid stained and topically colored. 6′ 10″ h x 32″ dia (each element).

Robert Teague

Tucson, Arizona, ironart57@yahoo.com

Artist's Statement

When creating a piece for someone, I try to make it reflect their personality and their environment. I believe this gives them a greater connection to the piece, as if they themselves had a part in the design.

Individual Artwork

Mirror Frame for Abram Whitaker

I designed and built this handmade frame for my nephew, Abram, as he began his new family.

Robert Teague. Mirror Frame for Abram Whitaker. Mild steel, solid copper cross pieces.

Doors for the Assini Family

Handmade doors for the Assini Family's Ranch, Cielo de los Caballos, "Horse Heaven."

Robert Teague. Doors. 2010.

Bert's Table

I made this table for my friend, Bert Seelman, of Performance Fitness Systems. He wanted a consultation table. Before I had completed the table, I took it by for Bert to see. He loved it so much he would not let me leave with it! I had to "steal" it when he was not looking so I could paint it and get the glass cut for it. I wondered for a moment whether I might not find myself in jail rather than getting paid for my work!

Robert Teague. *Bert's Table*. 2006. Mild steel, solid copper cross.

Jay Terry, Anthony Riley, and Dan Suffin

Oregon City, Oregon

Artist's Statement

Jay Terry, Anthony Riley, and Dan Suffin are the team at "CMS of Oregon, LLC," a small firm in Oregon City, Oregon, building custom gates and railings for customers in the Portland metropolitan area. We also endeavor to transform scrap metal into artistic pieces. We built a 23,000-pound machine that will twist any combination of materials up to twenty feet long. With this machine we have produced some fine art as well as opened a small market for custom twisted columns for architects and builders who desire a unique look and design.

Individual Artwork

Jay Terry, Anthony Riley, and Dan Suffin. Water fountain. Pond Railing. Fountain: 8" stainless steel. Railing: 1 1/4 steel pipe with powder coat finish.

Jay Terry, Anthony Riley, and Dan Suffin. Art Sculpture. 4″ square tube, powder coat finish.

Shelley Thomas

West London, United Kingdom, shelley@shelleythomas.co.uk

Artist's Statement

Inspiration comes primarily from my subconscious mind; what my senses have absorbed over the years constantly leads me to what I do and how I do it. On a conscious level I am directly influenced by what I see around me wherever I am. I look at and see the manmade more than the natural; I need a pylon or two to be marching across the countryside to grab my attention.

I am currently working on a new project, *Ferrous Road Kill,* using rusty pieces of steel I find in the street whilst out walking. I embellish these pieces with 22-carat gold and semi-precious stones.

Individual Artwork

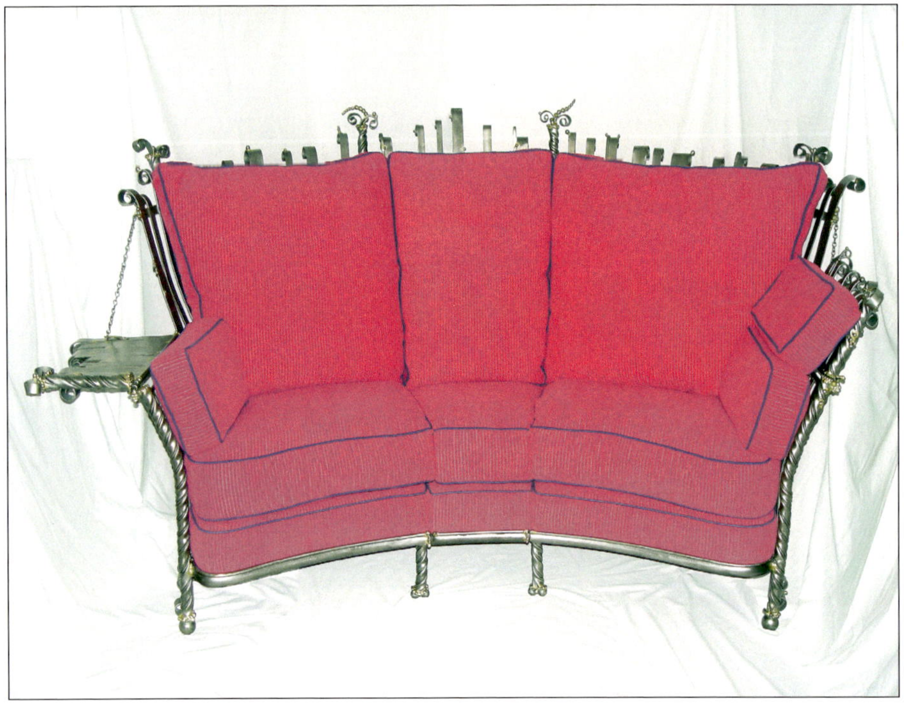

Shelley Thomas. *Dolly Sofa*. 3′ x 2′ 6″ x 3′.

Shelley Thomas. *Beverly's Staircase*.

Shelley Thomas. *Beverley's Gate*. 4′ x 6′.

Shelley Thomas. *Vester in Blue*. Veranda.

Shelley Thomas. *St. Margaret's Padlock Ferrous Road Kill.* Steel, 18-carat gold, amethyst, cubic zirconia, and garnet. 3″ x 2″.

Christopher Thomson

San Jose, New Mexico, susanctiron@gmail.com

Artist's Statement

I forge sculpture, architectural lighting, and home furnishings in white hot iron and bronze. Forms initially explored for their own sake find their way into my gates, railings, chandeliers, lamps, candlesticks, fireplace tool sets, tables, and chairs. Three employees and tools, from ancient to modern, help me with these creations. Life experiences subconsciously blend with the rich traditions of my craft to push the work in new directions.

Individual Artwork

Ranch Great Room Chandelier

An architect, with whom we had enjoyed successful collaborations in the past, told us he had a well traveled client wanting a forged three-tiered 10′ dia. x 11 1/2′ chandelier. He wanted the work to exude the primal immediacy of the best African tribal ironwork, while exhibiting the sophisticated nuances of eighteenth century French and Italian work. We forged the giant rings to cross-sections that were, by design, impossible to control. Vestigial remainders of fire and force and iron hit hot contrast nicely with the more polished voluptuous repoussé acanthus leaves. As the work progressed and was hung at finished height, interrelationships of form, light, and shadow, difficult to visualize from drawings, became apparent.

Designed, forged, and repoussé at Christopher Thomson Ironworks Studio in New Mexico. Collaboration with Curtis Windham Architects of Houston

Christopher Thomson. *Ranch Great Room Chandelier*. 2009. Forged steel and repoussé. The details show the middle and top tier acanthus leaf arms and candle cups. 10′ dia. x 11 1/2′ h. *Photos: Wendy McEahern* (above and opposite page)

Bird Wing Chandelier

Our studio had created and forged four custom-sized chandeliers previously for a designer's client in Dallas. The ceilings in that home were unusually low, so the chandeliers could not be taller than 14".

This same client requested a new chandelier be designed for her library using some of the design elements of the previously made chandeliers but with the addition of feathers. The four upholstered library chairs that sit under the chandelier sport exquisitely hand-carved wooden elongated bird wings for the arms that are gilt in silver.

Our priority objective was to create a chandelier that would capture a feeling of flight and complement the carved wooden arms of the four chairs.

Repoussé techniques on low carbon steel were used on the bird wings for this library chandelier. I contrasted the light flight-like graceful wings with the heavier forgings arranging the wings in a mandala pattern.

The artist/wood carver had made his work look like metal. I tried to maintain some of the qualities of carved wood in my repoussé work on the wings.

Designed, forged, and repoussé at Christopher Thomson Ironworks Studio in New Mexico.

Christopher Thomson. *Bird Wing Chandelier*. 2010. Forged steel and repoussé. 30" dia. x 14" h. *Photos: Susan Livermore*

Christopher Thomson. *Bird Wing Chandelier*. 2010. Forged steel and repoussé. 30″ dia. x 14″ h. *Photos: Susan Livermore*

Post Lantern

These hand-forged steel lanterns incorporate traditional blacksmithing techniques and joinery into a contemporary design and were created for lighting an estate in California.

The edges of the hoods are hammer thickened before being forged to shape hot and then riveted together. The ribs are hammered square from round stock acquiring the texture and variations of that process. Their bottom ends are upset to swell slightly and the tops are joined to the hood with tenons. Elegant but muscular design and joinery elements at the base of the post ensure stability and provide protection to the electrical box from weather. The clear crackled glass globes, hand-blown by a local craftsman, complement the aesthetic. At nightfall, the lanterns emit a warm golden glow welcoming those who walk the garden paths.

Designed and forged at Christopher Thomson Ironworks in New Mexico.

Christopher Thomson. *Post Lantern*. 2009. Forged steel + hand-blown clear crackle glass. 28″ h x 14″ dia. *Photo: Wendy McEahern* (opposite page)

Kenneth M. Thompson

Blissfield, Michigan, flatlandersculpture@netzero.net

Artist's Statement

I have long felt that profound art contained a high level of spiritual content, not necessarily that of religion, but that of the "spirit of a man," a spirit defined by his truth and honor. My sculpture is based on this form of spirituality.

Beyond content, my sculpture concentrates on the fundamental issue of form and how negative space defines it as well as the techniques employed to create it.

Individual Artwork

Steel Inverted

Kenneth M. Thompson. *Steel Inverted*. Pleasant Ridge, Michigan. 2006. Box built. Corten steel and limestone. 7′ x 6′ 6″ x 2′. *Photo: Bill Jackson*

Canton Community Arch

This piece serves homage to the agrarian past of Canton as it grows into a modern city.

Kenneth M. Thompson. *Canton Community Arch*. Canton Center Road & Ford Road, Canton, Michigan. 2006. Fabricated with 2″ x 2″ tube steel superstructure with applied skin. Corten steel, stainless steel, & limestone. 20′ x 20′ x 36′ (9,000 lbs).

Do Not Search For Profound Meaning In This Sculpture

Kenneth M. Thompson. *Do Not Search For Profound Meaning In This Sculpture*. ITC Building, Jackson Community College, Jackson, Michigan. 2007. Box built. Indiana Oolitic limestone & stainless steel. 3′ x 1′ 6″ x 6′ 6″ (1500 lbs.).

Hogan Arch

Commissioned to enhance the plaza and honor the retiring college president Saundra Tracy.

Kenneth M. Thompson. *Hogan Arch*. Hogan Center, Alma College, Alma, Michigan. 2009-10. Box built. Stainless steel with a Pennsylvania bluestone and nickel-plated ring set into the foundation. 12′ 6″ x 7′ x 3′.

Alumni Plaza

Commissioned to honor the alumni of the University of Toledo and their effect on the world.

Kenneth M. Thompson. *Alumni Plaza*. Corpus Christi University Parish, Toledo, Ohio. 2007-09. Fabricated with 2″ x 2″ tube steel superstructure with applied skin. Corten steel, stainless steel, Pennsylvania bluestone, limestone, concrete, and bricks. 26′ x 52′ x 3′.

Newton's Law Series: Junk Shot

Kenneth M. Thompson. *Newton's Law Series: Junk Shot.* 2010. Granite smashed fabricated steel. Steel and cast concrete. 1′ 6″ x 6′ 6″ x 10′ (800 lbs.).

Pavel Tovarek

Czech Republic, paveltovarek@seznam.cz

Individual Artwork

Pavel Tovarek. *Bird.* Miniature Sculpture. Forged. Steel. 4″ x 4″.

Pavel Tovarek. *Fish.* Sculpture. Steel. Forged. 4′ x 2′.

Pavel Tovarek. Indoors Railing. 1 1/4″ round solid steel center bars are from 1/2″ round steel. Beeswax finish. Private residence in the Czech Republic. 24′ long solid railing.

Pavel Tovarek. *Goblin.* Sculpture: "demon of alcohol." Forged. Steel. 17″ x 12″.

Pavel Tovarek. *Octopus.* Forged from plate. 4" x 3/4". 1' dia.

Pavel Tovarek. *Seahorse.* Forged and welded. Steel. 14″ x 6″.

Pavel Tovarek. *Twister.* Forged and twisted plate. 2′ x 1′.

Samuel Troxell

Tempe, Arizona, stroxell@asu.edu

Artist's Statement

My art seeks to bring out the beauty of the common, simple, or rustic. The Japanese term of "wabi" best grasps what I am after in my work. Wabi is beauty without gleaming color that is spiritual not sensory with a push towards the somber or subdued. Examples include random flowers growing among the weeds or the refreshing simplicity among earthly extravagance. In relations to my work it is the lasting mark of the hammer, the continuous thread in a weave, or the last iron leaf to a branch of steel.

Craftsmanship has become the foundation to my art as well as my search for perfection in a given task. Art has to take craftsmanship to a distinctly different form that is not obtainable in ordinary life. The level of craftsmanship developed by ancient cultures like the Japanese should be admired, and it is sad that such levels are not widely encouraged in this modern age. Metalsmithing needs a high level of craftsmanship due to the stubborn nature of the material. My work is both a marker of craft progression and a compass to my artistic future.

Individual Artwork

Memory of the North

Made in homage to my father, an Alaskan native, this piece brings memories of the time I spent with him. The Damascus is a star pattern layer twist of some 150 layers similar to the Turkish twist pattern. Stars on the top of the world look larger, and coupled with the sway of the northern lights gives rise to the pattern seen on the blade. Wenge wood native to Africa, not Alaska, with its deep, distinctive brown color reminds me of the coarse fur of the brown bear, which was a common sight to me when in the north. The shape off the blade is reliable, a knife that is used in hunting and fishing in the North Country.

Samuel Troxell. *Memory of the North.* Knife. 2009. Hand forged steel. Damascus steel, brass, and Wenge wood. 9" x 2" x 1". *Photos: Samuel Troxell*

Fisherman's Helper

This blade suits the function of a flaying knife. The intention is to bring up memories of fishing from the tying of a fly, to the fighting of the fish, and finally the cleaning of the catch. Often the knife is a forgotten element to fishing, being overshadowed by the fishing rod. Look closer and see the pool and flow of the stream in the pattern of the steel that symbolizes water.

The Damascus has been folded approximately 120 times, then twisted, and finally forged by hand. The blade is set within a wooden handle and sheath made of Leopard wood. The wood has an amazing likeness to the scales of a fish. Ornamented with a sterling silver hilt and wire wrapping brings distinguished breaks in the woodwork. The final touch of an attractive fly and hook forceps completes the memory of fishing adventures from start to finish.

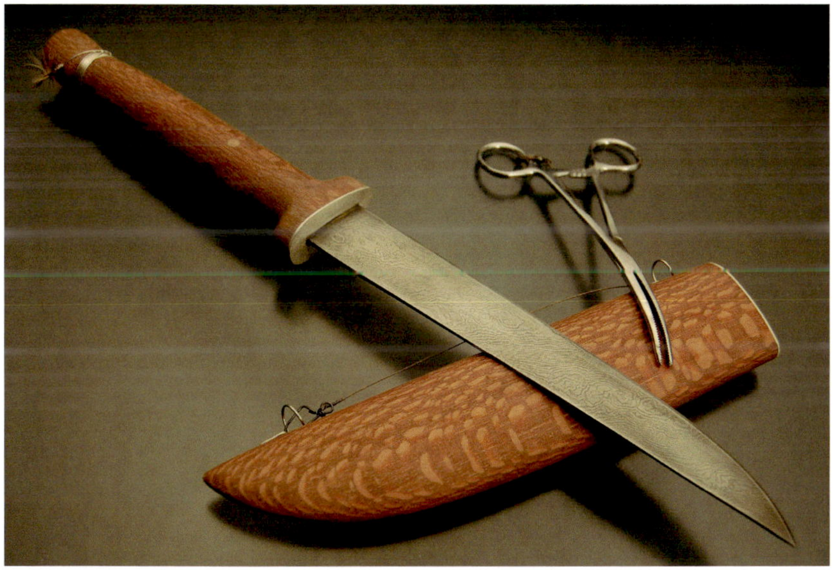

Samuel Troxell. *Fisherman's Helper.* Knife. 2010. Hand forged Damascus knife. Damascus steel, nickel, sterling silver, Leopard wood, found objects. 16" x 3" x 1". *Photos: Samuel Troxell*

Candle Cradle

The candle is suspended in a woven cradle of stainless steel keeping it protected from falling and yet also trapped. The light from the lit candle passes through the steel, reflecting the cage. The wax also passes through the woven walls, creating a new form drop by drop. The forged steel furnishing's aid in giving borders to the candleholder and makes it an interactive piece.

Samuel Troxell. *Candle Cradle.* 2010. Hand woven and forged construction. Stainless steel, steel, and wax. 8" x 6" x 5". *Photo: Tedd McDonah*

Jill Turman

Oakland, California, ironchick2@gmail.com

Artist's Statement

I am one of the lucky people who can honestly say that I love my job. In my studio, I get to use traditional blacksmithing techniques, industrial equipment, fire, and creativity to turn raw steel into art. It is always rewarding and often challenging. For me, blacksmithing is more than just hitting hot metal. I am a designer, a problem solver, an engineer, *and* a craftsman. Each project presents unique challenges and opportunities—this is what continues to inspire me.

Individual Artwork

Mesa Gate

This gate was designed for clients who love to travel in the Southwest. It functions as security and also as a partial windbreak for the passageway beyond. Open areas allow the homeowner to see out. The asymmetrical leaves of the gate allow the homeowner to open one side (3′ wide) for regular pedestrian use or both sides for moving larger yard equipment through the passageway.

Jill Turman. *Mesa Gate.* 2007. Hot formed and fabricated. Iron, copper, and stainless. 6′ 8″ h x 4′ 10″ w. *Photo: artist*

Garden Gate

A traditional style gate featuring snub end scrolls, collars, slit drifts, and a handmade gravity latch. The asymmetrical design suits the unusual opening between the side of the house and an old column.

Jill Turman. *Garden Gate*. 2008. Forged. Iron, painted faux finish. 5′ 8″ h x 3′ 6″ w. *Photo: Karna Kurata*

Fire Screen and Tools

The forged elements in this fire screen reflect the details in the mantle's stone carving. The open design is beautiful when not in use, but also allows the homeowner to see through the screen once a fire is built.

Jill Turman & Chris Winterstein. *Fire Screen and Tools*. 2008. Forged and fabricated. Iron. 3′ 6″ h x 3′ 6″ w. *Photo: Karna Kurata*

By the Letter

I was commissioned to design and build signs for the front and rear entries of the Firehouse Arts Center. Each letter features a textured/forged steel letter in front, a larger abraded stainless steel letter in back and LED rope lights between the two layers. The font and style of the signs was designed to be adapted into the facility logo and now appears on all publicity materials, letterhead, staff uniforms, etc.

Jill Turman. *By the Letter*. Signage for the Firehouse Arts Center, Pleasanton, California. 2010. Forged. Iron, abraded stainless steel, LED lighting. 18" h x 25' l. *Photo: artist*

Lyric: Firehouse Arts Center Donor Recognition Wall and Signage

In September 2010, the City of Pleasanton converted an old firehouse into a community art center featuring a 250 seat theater, gallery, and art studios. I received the commission to create a donor recognition wall for the lobby and signs for the front and back of the building.

The wall hung sculptural installation was designed to recognize financial contributors to the Firehouse Arts Center. The client requested "a donor recognition wall that we can add to over time and that doesn't look like a list." My response to their request is an art piece featuring gestural lines that invoke the idea of music, dance, and brush strokes. Donor's names are engraved on plaques and sprinkled across the piece.

Jill Turman. *Lyric.* Donor recognition plaques. Textured (forged) iron back plate and engraved brushed aluminum front plate. There are five different textures used for the iron back plates, designating five levels of financial contributions. (45+ donors are currently recognized on the wall.) *Photo: artist*

Jill Turman. *Lyric.* Donor Recognition Wall for the Firehouse Arts Center, Pleasanton, California. 2010. Forged. Iron and aluminum. 8′ h x 18′ l x 4″ d. *Photo: artist*

Eric Velleca

Loxahatchee, Florida, velleca@hotmail.com

Artist's Statement

The inspiration for most of my sculptural work seems to evolve from my interest in the relationships man has with nature, and nature has with man. Witnessing man's industrial genius and monumental accomplishments, as well as those of the natural world we are also a part of, my work serves as an instrument of observation and reaction. I enjoy visualizing the harmony and disharmony that exists between industry and nature, and how often these disharmonies are self-inflicted. And like everything in nature, it seems that the greater mass is a macro version of its microelements. In the same way, the horrible or great potential that man has shown in groups is inherently represented, at least in part, in all of us as individuals.

Individual Artwork

Teak Gate

This gate was commissioned upon the client approving the sample door pull. From there the design evolved. The door pull started as 2" square tapered at each end. Then it was twisted with local heats so as to counteract the metal's desire to twist at the tapers and not the fat part in the middle. After that, the ends were fullered and holes punched. The latch pulls were more of a challenge, as they needed to match, be heavy looking, and balanced so they are powered by gravity. I decided to make a similar twist as the pulls but split in half, thus keeping the more imposing scale of a larger twist but with reduced weight. Best of all, the hinge straps are actually holding the door, a rarity today.

Eric Velleca. *Teak Gate.* 2007. Forging, welding, bending, twisting. Steel, stainless steel, silicon bronze. 9.5' h x 8.5' w. *Photos: Eric Velleca*

Clocks #1

Clocks #1 was an idea I had for a few years. I am fascinated with time, fear wasting it, running out of it, and generally not having any control over it. I feel time will erase everything eventually. I made this clock for a showing of furniture made from mostly recycled materials. A friend gave me an old dumpster that provided the sheet steel. I went to the scrap yard for a few things and picked around my own scrap or leftovers as well. This clock design is based off Gothic architecture with the flying buttresses being utilized to seemingly suspend the clock and pendulum box. The chime vents at the top are loosely forge welded sprockets and scrap steel, and the door on the drawer at the bottom is solidly forge welded plate with sprockets, chain, nuts, and bolts. The compression of these industrial parts obscures them, giving them an archeological feel. The dumpster material, when sanded back, revealed the colors it had been painted through its life. These blues and greens look strikingly like planet Earth. I found it very gratifying to take elements that represent a few of the many great human accomplishments over time and rework them together while using or reusing materials and objects that are mundane, taken for granted, and/or discarded.

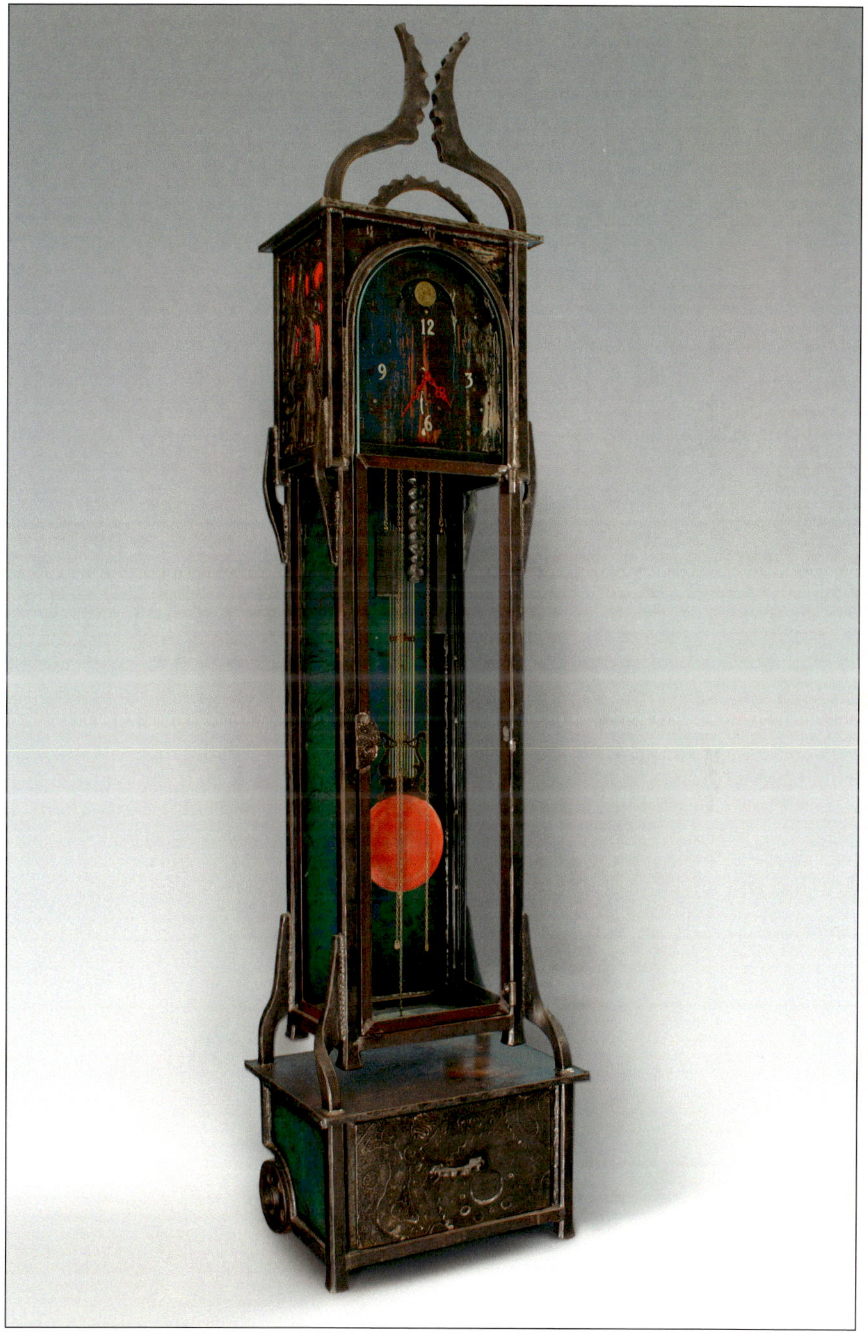

Eric Velleca. *Clocks #1.* 2008. Plasma cutting, forging, forge welding, machining, fabrication. Mild steel, found objects, fabric, clockworks. 106" h x 27" w x 18" d. *Photos: Ken Nelson*

Steel Dining Table

This table was inspired by Japanese wood furniture. The legs are 2" square bar punched and tenoned. The most difficult part of this table was making the top flat. I started out with a 5' x 5' x 1/2" thick plate. I naively expected the plate to stay reasonably flat after my initial straightening via wooden blocks and driving over it with a Case tractor. Then I torch cut the big square hole out of the middle. This is where things got severely challenging. I proceeded to clean the torch cuts and upset the edges of the inner square as well as the outer edges of the table with a hammer and torch. This heat seemed to contribute to severe warping of the plate. I first thought I might use heat and water to encourage a positive change. I learned a few things, one of them was how complicated this technique becomes when dealing with a huge, flat plain. In the end, I managed to get it as good as it looked before the heat and water technique. So I went to the press and decided to do it cold and with severe depth limitations as my press cannot reach into the middle of a 5' plate. Also, it was too heavy to carry and needed to be level at all times, and could not be set down on the press table without destroying the already upset edges. In the end, we got it flat, and in the future I would love to make another with a wood or glass top!

Eric Velleca. *Steel Dining Table.* 2008. Machining, fitting, forging, forge welding, sandblasting, patina finish. Mild steel, silicon bronze. 34" h x 60" w x 60" d. *Photos: Eric Velleca*

Gears #4

The *Gears* series is inspired by D & A and an industrial gear. The base is plate steel with stampings of gears reminiscent of an archaeological find. The gear strand is flat bar that has been fullered in graduating sizes as it tapers suggesting a finite lifetime middle age being the most robust.

Eric Velleca. *Gears #4.* 2008. Forging, stamping, sandblasting, painting. Mild steel. 27" h x 8" w. *Photo: Ken Nelson*

Interior Gate

Traditional design by the architect, David Gengler, created for an anonymous celebrity home.

Eric Velleca. *Interior Gate*. 2009. Forging, welding, gold leafing, sandblasting, painting. Mild steel, castings, catalog leaves. 90″ h x 35″ w. *Design by architect David Gengler. Photo: Eric Velleca*

Musical Railing

This railing was commissioned as a design based on an element available in catalogs of pre-made parts. As blacksmiths who work in the field of architectural ironwork, we are always connected in some way to our brothers, the out of a catalog fabricators of fine ironwork. The best part about this job was that the catalog element was actually kind of cool! Ironically, the most modern large railing I have done has been inspired by a catalog element! So I ran with it, scaled it up to a size that conveys as quality, and designed the rest to match it. Half way through, I realized why the client like this design so much. He is a musician, and the railing reads as sheet music. So I called him, and he started working on it. It is very interesting that the placement of the knots, or notes, was done at my discretion, as I found them pleasing visually. I am anything but musically inclined, but the client confirmed that it was composed very nicely and he translated it into a musical track illustrating the harmony of this convergence of these very different mediums.

Eric Velleca. *Musical Railing.* 2010. Forging, welding, sandblasting, painting. Mild steel. Approximately 60 linear feet. *Photo: Eric Velleca*

Joan Waters

Chandler, Arizona, joan@joanwaters.com

Individual Artwork

Joan Waters. *Rainforest Shield: Downpour.* 2006. Welded steel with patinas. 55″ x 30″ x 6″.

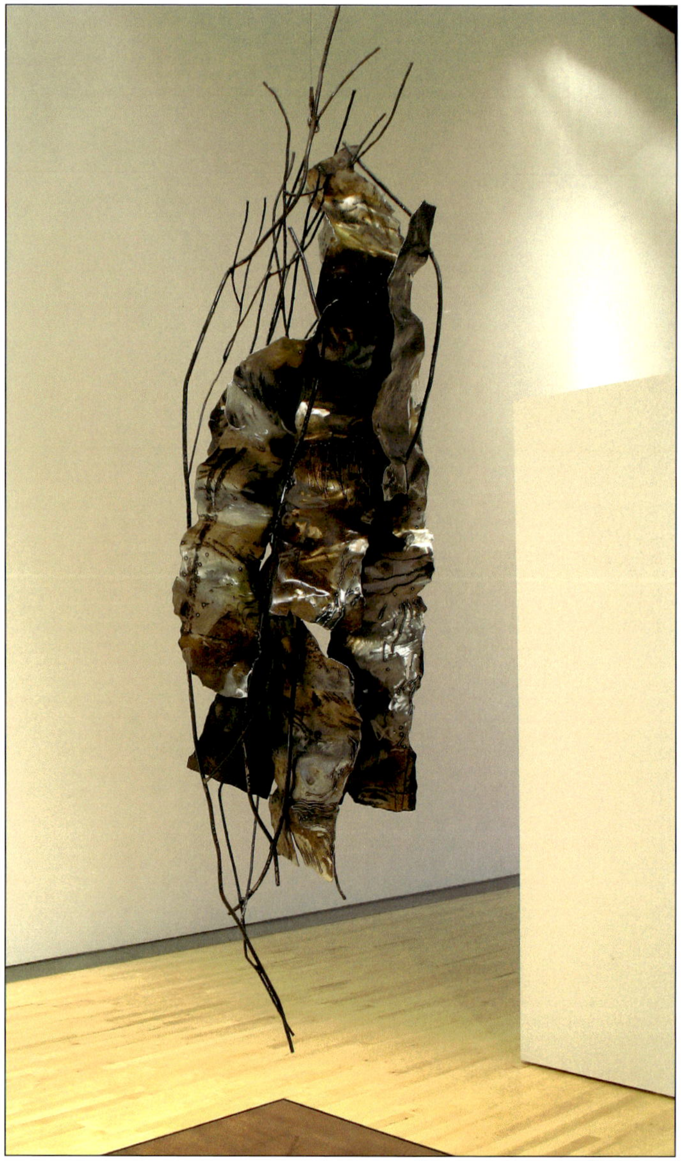

Joan Waters. *Transfiguration: Before There Was Green.* 2007. Welded steel with patinas. 84″ x 30″ x 32″.

Joan Waters. *Living Fossil (Horseshoe Crab).* 2009. Welded steel with patinas. 29″ x 16″ x 6″.

Joan Waters. *Treehouse.* 2010. Welded steel with patinas. 42″ x 19″ x 2″.

Joan Waters. *Under the Leafy Canopy.* 2010. Welded steel with patinas. 52″ x 14″ x 7″.

Joan Waters. *Before Flight.* 2010. Welded steel with patinas. 18″ x 21″ x 5″.

Ira R. Wiesenfeld

Tucson, Arizona, treeira@hotmail.com

Individual Artwork

Large Phoenix Nest Bowl

I began with railroad spikes, horseshoes, rebar, broken tools, leftover pipe, practice forgings, bolts, screws, and anything else I could find in my very large scrap pile. I left part of each element intact and forged the rest into wood textured branches with leaves, flowers, and pods as finials. I then welded the elements together into a vessel, sandblasted the whole piece, did a rust patina on the center, and shined the finials with a vine wheel. The center of the *Nest Bowl* shows the original material the element was forged from.

The theme of my *Phoenix Nest Bowl* is the history of the blacksmith as recycler. Steel used to be a precious commodity; it was not wasted. So, from the ashes of the scrap pile the Phoenix rises; new forms are created from old ones, and the cycle, or re-cycle, continues.

Ira R. Wiesenfeld. *Large Phoenix Nest Bowl*. 2010. Forged found steel objects, welded, sandblasted, partial rust, partial wire brush finish. 18" x 27" x 31". *Photos: David Harvey*

Bird of Paradise Lost

This piece has an environmental theme; if we don't start treating our Mother Nature better, she is going to mutate into some rather unpleasant forms. It came about when I looked at a bird of paradise flower and saw in it the blades of a knife.

I also made a similar piece from found objects that I call *Bird of Paradox*.

Ira R. Wiesenfeld. *Bird of Paradise Lost*. 2009. Forged steel and bronze, welded, sandblasted, partial black patina. 16" x 34" x 11". *Photo: David Harvey*

Hat and Cane Hall Tree

I make my hall trees to look like trees, twisted, gnarled, and textured like old wood. They are forged from solid steel stock, welded, and patinated.

The distinctive feature of this hall tree is that the hat and walking sticks are also forged and welded steel. It fooled most of the people who saw it at the 2009 Designer Showhouse, Tucson, Arizona, opening. They were surprised and delighted when I explained that the "accessories" were steel, and welded to the tree.

Ira R. Wiesenfeld. *Hat and Cane Hall Tree*. 2008. Forged and welded steel, black patina, paint, shell hatband. 68" x 18" x 16".

John Winer

Mountain City, Tennessee, john@laughingcrowforge.net

Artist's Statement

I am inspired by abstract forms as well as traditional motifs, and enjoy combining medieval joinery with a contemporary flavor. I like to ad lib around a specific form and try to capture an inspired emotion within the design.

The architectural framework of a piece becomes a canvas onto which I can paint an iron improvisation. Artistic blacksmithing is for me the place where Fire, Rhythm, Iron, and Ideas meet and cause a spontaneous combustion of my spirit that I can only watch manifest.

Individual Artwork

Interior Railing

Three berries and three small leaves create boughs on the vine work that adorns the tree-like railings.

John Winer. Interior Railing. Forged and fabricated. Mild steel. Linseed base coat and lacquer outer coat finish. *Photos: Reven T.C. Wurman of Wurman Studios.*

The Silent Rejoyce

This is a small, Art Nouveau style rail.

John Winer. *The Silent Rejoyce*. Railing. Forged. Mild steel traditionally joined Renaissance wax finish. *Photos: Reven T.C. Wurman of Wurman Studios.*

Welcome Night and Day

In this driveway gate, a fiery sun is depicted in the west and a wispy moon in the east.

John Winer. *Welcome Night and Day.* Traditionally joined with fabricated welds hidden under the collars. Mild steel. Scale is left on the steel, then acid treated and coated with a spar urethane. *Photos: Reven T.C. Wurman of Wurman Studios.*

Haley Woodward

Austin, Texas, halingwdwang@hotmail.com

Artist's Statement

At the core, my work is rooted in a fascination with the dynamic qualities of heated steel. As steel consumes heat, it comes alive. The steel increasingly gains incandescence and elasticity until the moment when solid steel becomes liquid. The ability to control this transformation is a constant source of enthrallment to me. Simultaneously when the steel is active, it is nearly unapproachable. The extreme temperatures force one to manipulate steel with harder metal extensions. Although the metal is heated, it requires great force to move. The force applied must be precise and controlled. Because the material will only stay active for a limited time without reheating, everything needs to happen with deft precision. Depending on the size of the work, multiple smiths may labor together on one project, allowing opportunities for collaboration. Some collaborations are creative, and others simply physical. Creative collaborations involve sharing ideas and perspectives, technically and conceptually. Physical collaborations involve the material objective and what it will take to realize the final project. When working this way, wonderful moments of nonverbal communication occur, where words are replaced with mirrored movements and hand signals. The dance that ensues is an art of its own as far as I am concerned. This dance is something that I have found moving and beautiful since I was first exposed to it. All of these factors, from the changing characteristics of steel to the physical act of moving the metal with hammer and anvil, create a working environment that is mentally and physically challenging and rewarding.

Individual Artwork

Haley Woodward. *It Only Lives In Space.* Sculpture. Forged and fabricated. Steel, stainless steel. 19″ x 15″ x 20″. *Photo: Brian Morrison*

Haley Woodward. *Root 3015.* Forged and fabricated. Steel, stainless steel. 3′ x 4′. *Photo: Brian Morrison*

Haley Woodward. *DwangBot 06.* Sculpture with freestanding feet. 2006. Forged and fabricated. Steel, copper. 30″ x 14″ x 20″. *Photo: Brian Morrison*

Haley Woodward. *Dark Space Explorer.* Wall mounted sculpture. 2009. Forged and fabricated. Steel. 24″ x 10″ x 9″. *Photos: Brian Morrison.*

Haley Woodward. *Deep Sea Stacey.* Sculpture. 2008. Forged and fabricated. Steel. 10″ x 8″ x 5″. *Photo: Brian Morrison*

Wyoming Metalsmiths

Cowley, Wyoming, Rik@WyomingMetalsmiths.com

Artist's Statement

Nature, Native American art, and most of a lifetime of working with horses and cattle, mixed with a deep appreciation of the work of the great masters inspires us. However, we do think that imitating others stifles creativity, so we believe that one should follow one's own path. And we believe that the pathway to good design is found through the old methods.

Individual Artwork

Wyoming Metalsmiths. Twisted Bistro Table. Organic iron base with foot rest, transitioning into twisted dwarf cedar, supporting a traditional quatrefoil tabletop with glass overlay. 38" tall.

Wyoming Metalsmiths. Granite Top Bistro Table. Organic base transitioning into 3′ of iron rope supporting the granite top. 40″ h, 205 lbs.

Wyoming Metalsmiths. Art Deco Lamp. Body twisted from 5 solid 1″ bars. 26″ tall, 25 lbs.

Wyoming Metalsmiths. 2″ Iron Rope Bar Foot Rail with matching bar top brackets. Restaurant in Sheboygan, Wisconsin. *Photo: Matt Moeller*

Jason The York

Victor, Iowa, The.york@hotmail.com

Artist's Statement

The time and struggle of making an object is every bit as important as the finished piece. In our "click and ye shall receive" society, it is unique and comforting to have the ability to actually create something. There is a freedom and satisfaction involved in making that, sadly, many people never take the time to experience.

Individual Artwork

Untitled

This table served as an exploration of the hierarchy of importance. Tabletops are generally considered the most important part of the table. However, they often don't get the decorative touches that grace the rest of the table. If the tabletop is the most important functionally, should it not also be the most important visually?

Jason The York. *Untitled.* 2008. Forged, formed, fabricated. Mild steel, wood, Damascus, brass. 25" x 20" x 20". *Photos: George Ensley Photography*

Doggie Door

During a slow time at work, my employer gave me the opportunity to create a door so the studio dogs could get some fresh air. At the time I was experimenting in art nouveau and came up with this as a result.

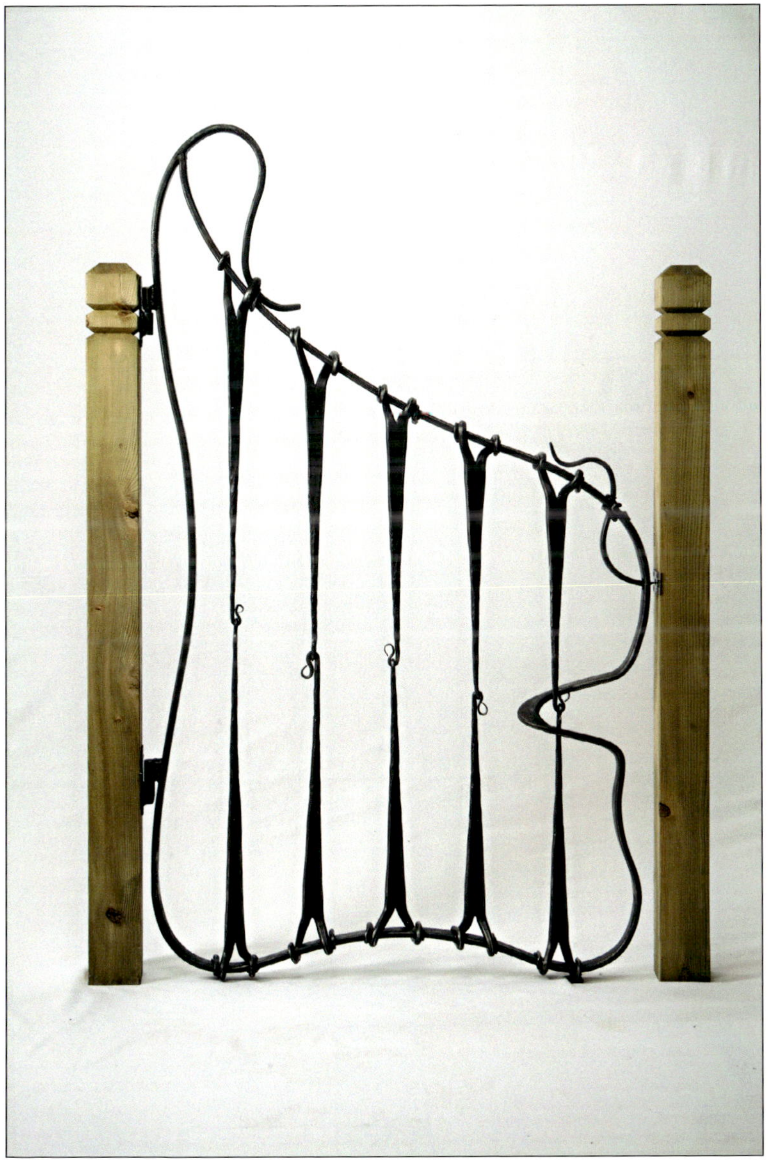

Jason The York. *Doggie Door.* Forged, formed, fabricated. Mild steel. 58" x 36" x 2.5". *Photo: Wendy Griffith*

DImascus

Jason The York. *DImascus*. 2009. Forge welded, fabricated. 5/8" x 5/8" x 5/8". *Photo: George Ensley Photography*

Stuck-up South Beach Sea Sponge

The piece was made in response to a recent visit to south beach.

The people of south beach, beautiful you are
With your tan bodies and expensive clothes
Strutting your stilettos, driving nice cars
You are dressed to the nines striving to show

Spiky hair, tight shirts, certainly a "Bro"
Your bright white shoes will nearly blind a man
Aimlessly circling walking to and fro
Brand new holey faded jeans, perfect tan

How can you see always in sunglasses?
How can you sense and feel in those high heels?
Can you hear when earth and ipod clashes?
Nose so high, can you even nasal feel?

You're a counterfeit, nothing but a lie
You cannot even look me in the eye

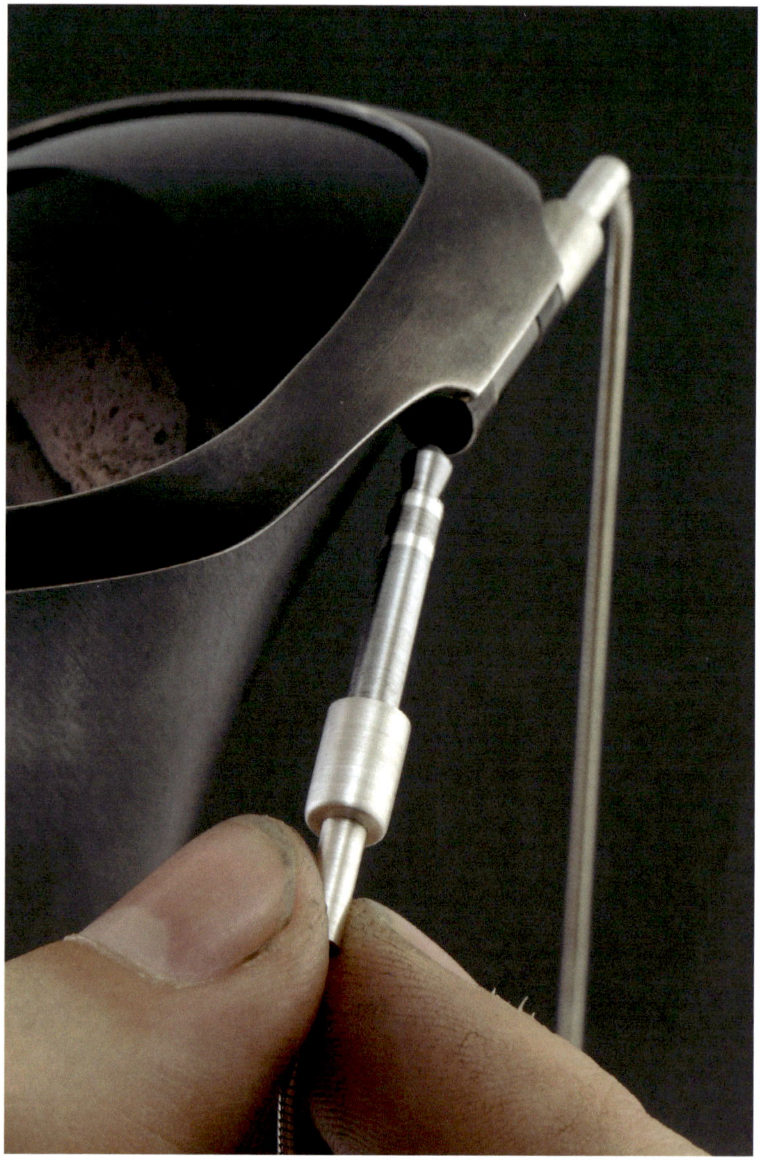

Jason The York. *Stuck-up South Beach Sea Sponge*. 2010. Forged, fabricated. 10" x 3.5" x 3.5". *Photos: George Ensley Photography* (right and opposite page)

Stephen Yusko

Cleveland, Ohio, syusko@sbcglobal.net

Artist's Statement

The objects I make are an exploration of form, line, surface, and function. They're also the result of my appreciation and fascination with materials—specifically with steel. Whether used alone or with other materials, I'm drawn to the industrial history of steel, its working properties, structural shapes, methods of joinery, and the way it patinas with age.

Frequently an idea starts with salvaged materials that I deconstruct. I enjoy the challenge in creating joinery solutions that become a key element of design. The clean, simplicity of the design often belies the complexity that is achieved only through a thorough understanding of the material.

Individual Artwork

Stephen Yusko for Rose Iron Works. *Squashed Block Oil Lamp*. Forged and fabricated. Steel, stainless steel, glass tube, wick. 3 3/4" x 2 5/8" x 2 5/8". *Photo: Dan Morgan*

Stephen Yusko for Rose Iron Works. *Console Table.* 2009. Forged and fabricated. Steel, stainless steel, Corian. 32" x 46" x 16 1/2". *Photo: Dan Morgan*

Stephen Yusko. *Nine Square Box.* 2010. Forged and fabricated. Steel. 5 1/4″ x 3 1/2″ x 3″. *Photo: Dan Morgan*

Stephen Yusko. *Yellow Box Series* (3 boxes). 2010. Forged and fabricated. Steel. 4 1/4″ x 3″ x 3″. *Photo: Dan Morgan*

Stephen Yusko. *Squashed Teapot.* 2010. Forged and fabricated. Steel. 4 1/2″ x 5″ x 2 3/4″. *Photo: Jeff Bruce*

Stephen Yusko. *Nine Square Oil Can.* 2010. Forged and fabricated. Steel. 8″ x 5 1/2″ x 2 3/4″. *Photo: Dan Morgan*

Index